THE AIR IN THE ROOM

THE AIR IN THE ROOM
A REPORT FROM THE SIXTIES

LSD
**WILLIAM BURROUGHS &
SCIENTOLOGY**

THE END OF PORN
THE END OF SUBSTANCE ABUSE
THE END OF NATIONALISM
THE END OF RELIGION
THE END OF SELF-IMPORTANCE
THE END OF SIGNIFICANCE
WHERE THE ACTION IS

BY GEORGE D. ROLLINS III

S-H Publishing
First Published in the United States by Zola Rollins, S-H Publishing.

Copyright © 2025 by George Rollins
No part of this publication may be reproduced, distributed, or transmitted in any form or by any means, including photocopying, recording, or other electronic or mechanical methods, without the prior written permission of the publisher, except as permitted by U.S. copyright law.

All rights reserved.

Title: The Air in the Room: LSD, William Burroughs & Scientology
ISBN: 979-8-9986861-0-8 (hardback)
979-8-9986861-1-5 (paperback) 979-8-9986861-2-2 (e-book)
Names: George Rollins / Author
A.O. Thomas / Editor
Norma Jean Rollins / Editor

Cover art by George Rollins
Cover design by Zander Raymond
Book design by Zola Rollins
Photo (dedication page) by Julia Kuskin
Photo (hardback jacket) by Thomas Antel

First edition 2025
Library of Congress Control Number: 2025911071

DEDICATED TO OUR SONS AND DAUGHTERS
AND GRANDCHILDREN.
AND TO EVERYONE WHO WAS THERE.

CONTENTS

INTRODUCTION
Childhood 1
Boarding School 11
University 15
Photographs 1948-1966 **19**

WILLIAM BURROUGHS & SCIENTOLOGY
A First Hand Account 29
New York and Ithaca 31
Meeting William Burroughs 37
What Is Auditing? 41
Finding Out Who This William Was 51
Saint Hill and Chillingstreet Cottage 57
The summer of 1968 65
Burroughs' Interest in Scientology 69
The Beginning of the End 77
Scientology's Concept of Ethics 81
From England to New York and Out to LA 89
The Bunker and Beyond 99
Photographs 1967-2017 **109**
Correspondance 1969-1989 **125**

LSD...WAKING UP
1966 - The Trip That Changed Everything 137

THE BIRDS AND THE BEES AND THE BURNING BUSH
The Reason for Being 147
Ordinary Sexual Orgasm 151
Extra-Ordinary Non-Sexual Orgasm 155
Where the Action Is 161

PREFACE

It is no secret that the mid-1960s were a pivotal time of unprecedented social change, and for many of us who were there, a moment of great promise and awakening. With the aid of LSD and other psychedelics, we bid farewell to 1950s America and came face to face with a new reality in which a very special light permeated the universe, connecting all things.

In spite of the miraculous and totally unforeseen nature of my own experience, which I will detail later, I don't believe that my story would be particularly unique except for the fact that in the fall of 1967 I had the good fortune to meet William Burroughs. And even though this encounter and ensuing friendship may not prove to be particularly significant to anyone other than myself, I still feel compelled to leave a first-hand account for those of you who are interested in those times and in this seminal, enigmatic figure of late 20th century literature and culture.

THE AIR IN THE ROOM

INTRODUCTION
CHILDHOOD

At the risk of telling you more than you might care to know, I am going to provide you with some context. I want to give you some idea of what those times and my own circumstances were like so that you might better understand what happened.

My birth certificate states that I was born in 1944 not far from New York City. Sixteen months later my brother was born, and not long after that our father moved the two of us and our mother out into the New Jersey countryside near his mother's house — about an hour's drive northwest of his office which was just across the Hudson from Manhattan.

What memories I have of my early childhood are

generally pleasant, but not without an undercurrent of melancholy and uncertainty. I recall having had a tendency to occasionally burst into tears without a great deal of provocation.

I grew up in a fairly large, solidly built two-story house located on Main Street in a small town surrounded by rolling hills, woodlands, and dairy farms.

This piece of property had a large and secluded backyard shaded by beautiful old trees. It also contained a perfusion of cascading honeysuckle, lilacs, roses, and two long peony beds which in springtime provided magnificent flowers that our mother cut and arranged in one or two vases around the house — especially on weekends when our father drove out from the city.

He was a handsome and charming, impeccably dressed man then in his early forties. He had established his own successful business — pioneering mobile chest x-ray surveys, primarily screening for tuberculosis. As a small child I admired him, looked up to him, and loved to occasionally get to wrestle-around with him, but he was always somewhat of a mystery and I can't say that I ever really got to know him.

On most Saturday nights he took our mother out to Perona Farms, one of the area's very few fancy restaurants. A babysitter from the neighborhood, usually Mrs. Ellis, would come over and look after my brother and me. On Monday mornings after breakfast he drove back into the city.

Although our father was a very significant part of our lives and set his own unspoken standards, my brother and I were in fact raised by our mother. She was born in 1907, the youngest of ten children. She weighed two and a half pounds at birth and was incubated in a basket placed on the oven door in the family kitchen. As a young girl she was tall and thin and grew up fairly poor in Arkansas, something our father would occasionally, if somewhat good-naturedly, tease her about. But by the time they met she'd become a registered nurse and anesthetist, working in a major New York area hospital. When I was born, Mom gave up her job nursing. She was 37 years old and when we moved to the country, she did not know how to drive a car.

To say that I was close to my mother would be an understatement. She was there when I woke up every morning, she dressed me, made breakfast, lunch, and dinner and that was everyday. She was loving and caring and easy-going. She supervised my play and managed to keep me from breaking my long-suffering younger brother's neck.

I remember sitting halfway down the basement stairs on a cold winter morning watching her shovel coal from the coalbin into the furnace. When the house was modernized, this system was replaced with an automatic oil burner.

As my brother and I grew older, the three of us would occasionally walk uptown to take in an early movie.

We strolled easily in the golden light of late afternoon along sidewalks lined with huge old maple trees and well established homes. At that time this small town had two theaters and going to the movies was always a treat — the dimming lights, the graceful, majestic parting of the stage curtains, the big red circle at the beginning of the Tom and Jerry cartoons filling the screen.

This seemed to be a world of safety and innocence where we could play unattended for hours in the backyard, venturing into the adjacent pine grove, and later into the nearby woods. While my brother and I certainly did our share of exploring and bike-riding around the neighborhood, we generally stayed pretty close to home — building forts, climbing trees, and playing Cowboys and Indians. At the end of the day if we still happened to be outside, our mother would stand at the back door and call us into dinner. Except on weekends, it was just the three of us. Her cooking was simple and straightforward and because of her Arkansas upbringing, had a southern tinge — she really knew how to fry chicken.

It is now difficult even for me to believe that this was a time just before the advent of television and Mom put us to bed early. Although I sometimes resisted these early bedtimes, the upside was that in the morning I felt wonderfully rested and very very good. On those rare occasions when I happened to wake up before she had, I'd run into her room and jump into bed with her for a few moments before the day officially began.

As you might imagine, come November the idyllic summers of northern New Jersey ended abruptly and it was not long before Dad decided to move the family to warmer climes during winter's cold and snowy months. To accomplish this move, Mom had to learn to drive, and although she became a competent driver, she was never truly comfortable doing it.

Our destination and my winter home from 1947 until 1957 turned out to be a sleepy little farming community in southeastern Florida about halfway between Miami and Palm Beach. This small town sat alongside the major north-south railroad tracks and Old Dixie Highway. It was also located about two and a half miles inland from some of America's most beautiful beaches. In those days these beaches were essentially deserted. I guess the farmers did not have the time or the inclination to go to the beach and consequently, at least in the beginning, almost no oceanfront development had taken place. There were, however, some beachfront cottages along A1A that had been built by the Kester Brothers to accommodate tourists and we rented one of them. There was strict segregation in the South at that time and years later I realized that Old Dixie Highway was the dividing line between black and white.

After a few winters we moved several blocks north into a small two-bedroom house also owned by the Kesters at 1100 N. Ocean Boulevard. It was off by itself on a big sandy lot. Around it grew a few coconut palms and large Spanish Bayonets. Out the backdoor looking east, there was a sand dune overgrown by a thick stand of sea grape trees. As you approached these trees, a branch-covered, tunnel-like path appeared as if by magic. Going up this path maybe fifteen yards, you emerged atop the dune looking out over the Atlantic Ocean, the Gulf Stream not far off shore. This view was fascinating, ever changing, and on occasion truly breathtaking — dead-flat-calm and sparkling in morning sunlight. And the water was warm, and we pretty much had it all to ourselves.

Dad periodically flew down out of Idyllwild on Eastern for two or three weeks at a time, especially around Christmas and Easter. We were always excited to see him. Our parents had friends who vacationed in the area and they all seemed to enjoy themselves when they got together. Cocktails were definitely on the agenda.

If my brother or I ever got sick, our mother called Dr. Windsor. He was Old Pompano and then some. He seemed elderly, slightly frail, and wore wire-rimmed glasses. He was fair-skinned and always dressed completely in black — including a black, broad-brimmed hat like a cowboy hat but the crown more flattened and the brim more rounded. He carried a black doctor's bag and always came to our house. Dr. Windsor had a glass hypodermic needle, and a shot of penicillin seemed to be his go-to cure for just about everything. I later learned that he had practiced in India for many years before settling in Pompano.

Occasionally Mom drove from the beach across the narrow steel-girder swing-bridge to the Piggly Wiggly market for groceries and to the Helpy Selfy — a long and low metal-roofed, semi-open-air affair located on the southside of Atlantic Boulevard around the corner from the town's three block-long business district which faced the railroad tracks and Old Dixie Highway to the west.

The Helpy Selfy featured damp concrete floors with cement troughs and washers along both side walls. The top half of these walls were simply open to the outside. The whole place smelled of laundry soap and humidity. The washing machines were basically enameled tubs on four legs — Maytags with ringers on top through which Mom put the clothes after washing and rinsing to squeeze out the water. There were no dryers. Even years later, long after Maytag had stopped making them, she continued to swear by this kind of washer.

Each spring Mom loaded the car and we began the three and sometimes four day trip back up the east coast along US Route 1. As she had just learned to drive, this was a somewhat harrowing endeavor for her. After an introductory expedition with our father, she did all the driving herself, initially in a gigantic gray 1948 four-door Packard sedan with standard shift on the column. She was terrified of having to stop on a hill and once while trying to cross a steep bridge in traffic near Charleston, South Carolina, she threw in the towel and after setting the emergency brake, got out of the car and asked a nearby driver to help her get the car moving again.

The overall road conditions, especially in the southern

states, were not good. Mostly poorly maintained two-lane blacktop. The occasional sight of crews of Black men chained together at the ankles and working along the roadsides was puzzling and unsettling. The men in these chain gangs wore black and white, broadly-striped, loose-fitting clothing, and were supervised by uniformed guards on horseback, cradling shotguns.

This was a time well before the Interstate Highway System had been built and there was none of the predictability and false sense of security provided by today's sanitized and ubiquitous chain infrastructure. As you traveled, whatever you happened to encounter in the way of services was a true reflection of the time, the place, and the local people, and you took your chances. In spite of these conditions, and even with two small boys often fighting and whining and jumping-around all over the back seat of the car, she always made it.

One of the most unpleasant and unforeseen moments in what in retrospect appears to have been a fairly idyllic childhood occurred when I first realized that "going to school" would require me being out of arm's reach of my mother. I knew intuitively that this was not going to be a good thing and by and large until I entered college it really wasn't. After an early and mercifully brief encounter with public schools, which I found disorienting and somewhat frightening, the remainder of my education took place in private schools.

Eventually Dad bought a small house in the area, a block

and a half from the beach. He had good taste in design and furnishings and it seemed that almost overnight this place was transformed from a somewhat nondescript, single-story cinder block structure on a flat sandy lot into a modest but elegant little home. Before long the back yard even included a small swimming pool. I vaguely recall the entire lawn, trees and much of the other landscaping appearing in what seemed like a single day. When we returned home from school one afternoon, it was all there, done.

Mom got us up every morning and made breakfast which often consisted of Bisquick pancakes with butter and maple syrup, and one half of an eight ounce bottle of Coca Cola each. Guided by the design in the glass bottle, she would pour the top half of the Coke into a cup for my brother, and I guess being the eldest, I was given the remaining half in the chilled bottle. Mom had been 18 years old when she first encountered Coke and she never looked back.

After breakfast she drove us to our nearby country day school and picked us up in the afternoon. There was a hand-cranked two-lane swing-bridge along A1A which we had to cross on our way to and from school. Sometimes, especially in the morning, we might "get the bridge," as it had been opened to allow sportfishing boats to exit the Intercoastal Waterway to the open ocean. While we were waiting for the bridge to be closed, Mom occasionally allowed my brother and me to get out of the car so we could get a better look at the boats as they went by. When the tide was high, the water was crystal clear with hundreds of colorful tropical fish swimming about the pilings. Crossing this bridge, there was an unobstructed view of Lighthouse Point maybe a quarter mile to the east. I would try to judge the ocean's mood by the size and nature of the waves at the mouth of the inlet.

As I grew older I became aware of new clouds on the horizon. I had by now of course heard the talk of total nuclear annihilation and seen the flickering images of hatred on our small black and white TV screen during the McCarthy Hearings and sensed the fear. But more worrying to me personally was the gathering understanding that I would be attending boarding schools in the Northeast from the eighth grade on. At the time of this realization I must have been about twelve years old and even though I was not quite as close to my mom as I had been as a small child, I was not looking forward to my imminent separation from her, and although she did not or could not intervene, I could tell that she was not that happy about it either.

BOARDING SCHOOL

In the fall of 1958 my introduction to the world of suit-and-tie, Northeastern boarding school education began and I hated it from the beginning. It was drudgery — somehow false and hypocritical and academically mostly about memorization. The headmaster had absolute power and if a student crossed one of the many lines drawn within this insular society, he found himself on the first available train home, baggage to follow. The regimentation and conformity demanded were suffocating, and although this was not a religious school, students were required to attend chapel every evening before dinner and a full service on Sunday mornings. My parents had not been churchgoers so this was my introduction to organized religion, and I found it boring, uninspiring, self-serving, and in a word — dead.

And if all of the above weren't bad enough, there were absolutely no girls at this school — none — anywhere. As I progressed further into my teens, I found this situation to be extremely unwelcome and my estrangement from summer romance less and less bearable. I boycotted the occasional, arranged dances with nearby girls' schools finding them degrading and ridiculous — and very well supervised.

There were, however, some positive things that occurred during this, my incarceration in the frozen north. I had loved rock and roll since the first time I'd heard Elvis singing "Heartbreak Hotel" and his early music had been my first inkling that "somethin' was goin' on." And it was during this lock-up period that I began to learn how to play the electric guitar. Although I had no specific musical gifts, I did develop some skills, and music would go on to play an important, if secondary, role in my life.

I also formed a close relationship with Karl Pacanovsky, the cantankerous and uncompromising old-world craftsman who was the head of the school's Arts and Crafts Department. Born in Slovakia and already an accomplished craftsman and wood carver restoring cathedral altars in Vienna, as a young man of eighteen walked to Hamburg where, on an impulse, he caught a boat to the States a few years before the outbreak of the First World War. When I met him he had a full head of white hair, sideburns, a mustache, and burning eyes that could look right through you.

Freshman year, after a compulsory, introductory exposure to this department, which also included fine arts and a metal shop, ninety-nine percent of the incoming students found this man to be so thoroughly intimidating and demanding that they stayed as far away from him and his woodshop as they could get. Consequently, over a four year period, in what little spare time I had, he became my private tutor and mentor. He encouraged me to design, and taught me how to build real furniture. He also taught me the rudiments of drafting and mechanical drawing. These abilities and my observation of his fierce attention to detail would serve me well all my life.

In ending my account of this frustrating and annoying boarding school interlude, let me say that I made only one friend among the students at this awful place, and this young man took his own life sometime in the early 1980s. Although we had not stayed in constant close communication during the ensuing years, we were very definitely in touch and I could not have been more surprised or perplexed on hearing this news.

UNIVERSITY

In the fall of 1963 my fortunes took a totally unforeseen turn for the better. For reasons that are still not completely clear to me, I found myself enrolled as a freshman in the fine arts department of one of the Ivy League universities. This world was the flip side of what I had just suffered through. There was total, unrestricted and unsupervised freedom. I had already satisfied most of my academic necessities in boarding school, so after taking a few required classes in the first term of my freshman year, I was able to devote myself completely to my art classes. I did not find these classes terribly taxing and generally enjoyed them. I usually got very high marks and my father, who kept track of these things, was always pleased to inform me when I'd "made the dean's list." My mom was happy that I was happy. And there was no shortage of delightful young women at this institution of higher learning.

Just before wrapping up this introduction, let me say emphatically that at this point in my young life I was essentially very much asleep as a spiritual being. I was unaware of being aware and was not able to contact other human beings in a direct or meaningful way.

This was the time when marijuana and psychedelic drugs first hit northeastern college campuses, and I loved being at ground zero. By the fall of 1964 I was well on my way to having shoulder-length hair, and soon became a member of the area's first home-grown rock and roll band. We played around the university at frat houses, in local bars, at the town's namesake hotel, and on nearby campuses. We even booked a couple of gigs in New York City.

Our small group of would-be artists and musicians lived off campus in rented farm houses and tarpaper shacks. During my junior and senior years I lived in a former one-room schoolhouse replete with two giant blackboards and a wall of 10-foot tall, double-hung windows. An indoor hand pump provided the water. The rent was fifteen dollars a month. We did artwork, smoked pot, dropped acid, and listened hard to the music that was emerging. This one time school house also served as our band's practice space.

I spent a couple of summers hitchhiking around Europe, sleeping by the side of the road, crashing in abandoned buildings, and occasionally staying with young acquaintances I'd gotten to know along the way while playing guitar and singing on the streets for spare change. Young people like these new friends I made in 1964 were the leading edge of a movement that would soon spread around the western world and beyond.

As you may have surmised by now, at this point my young life could not have been much better or more exciting, and yet there was still, beneath it all, a mildly nagging, difficult-to-define melancholy and uncertainty, a feeling of uneasiness, and a vague but persistent underlying sense of confusion. On very rare occasions there were even brief outbursts of ill-tempered aggressiveness.

Astonishingly, just as I was about to enter my senior year of art school, this unpleasant state of being came to a totally unforeseen and abrupt end one September evening in 1966 in New York City. This profound change of mind was precipitated by a single LSD trip which I will go on to describe in some detail. For the moment however I will simply note that it was this experience that would not only change my life completely but which would lead me directly to William Burroughs almost exactly one year later and that this meeting was one of the most important events in my life—especially so in the context I am about to describe.

**PHOTOGRAPHS
1948-1966**

Our Family in Pompano, c. 1948

Kester Cottages, Pompano Beach Florida c. 1940's

Our family at the train stop, on the west side of the main drag. I have no recollection of whom we were meeting.

The main drag in old Pompano circa 1950. The Railroad tracks and Old Dixie Highway just out of frame to the right.

This photo was taken around 1950 during the Main Street kitchen remodel. I think the body language says about all you need to know about my relationship with my mother.

My parents occasionally went to Varadero, Cuba before the revolution c.55 a stamp on the back of the card reads: Estudios Victor Fotografias Mar 6, 1955 and in my mother's handwriitng: Gertrude & Dayton Veradero, Cuba

This is exactly what Hillsboro Inlet looked like when we crossed the manually operated swingbridge to and from school in the 1950s. The lighthouse appears to be getting a coat of primer before a new coat of its iconic black and white.

Boarding school year book photo 1963.

    The thing that I find so interesting about this highly stylized photo is that in many ways it perfectly represents that "frozen moment in time" (Burroughs' phrase) when the seismic shift I write about in this report was about to take place. Currently I believe we are experiencing the death throes of the reality that was largely replaced in the 1960s and 70s. It has taken over sixty years for this final convulsion, this extinction burst to occur. And although this chaotic situation may not end quickly, it will end. Don Juan might have called this a shift in the Tonal of the Times, defined in part as the collective societal norms and/or the agreed upon reality which in part create our perception of the world in which we find ourselves.

Mojos 1964 -1966

This photo was taken by an unknown photographer probably in the late fall of 1964 at the Hofbrau bar and restaurant on College Avenue a couple of blocks south of the main entrance to the Cornell campus in Ithaca, New York. Midwinter of the previous semester Steve Newhouse, in the white shirt, decided to put a band together and asked Eric Stand, far left, playing bass and yours truly on rhythm and vocals to join him. Steve was a talented guitar player and vocalist who could sing harmony. Although Eric had never played bass before, at one time he was ranked number three on the violin in the thirteen and under division in New York City and he thought he could pick it up pretty easily and he did. He also helped out on the vocals. Steve was the band leader and came up with the name Mojos.

Newspaper Ad Fall 1964

We thought we were pretty dangerous. From left: our first drummer, whose name regretfully eludes me, yours truly, Eric Stand, and Steve Newhouse. We're standing at the roof's edge of a very funky tarpaper shack that a classmate and I had rented the second year of college. It was about four miles north of the Cornell campus on Burdick Hill Road just off North Triphammer Road. This area was mostly farmland and countryside then.

We picked up a great drummer named Sonny Coleman (center) later that year. He was a townie and told us that at the time he was working in a local salt mine and that he didn't care for it. (I had no idea such mines existed in that area.) In 1966 Bill Buckman joined us on keyboard. He was a great addition, no photo unfortunately.

Photo for combined art and architecture show at Cornell, 1966.
Far left, Robin Williams (no relation), myself in the middle and seated next to me on my left, Sue Rothenberg.

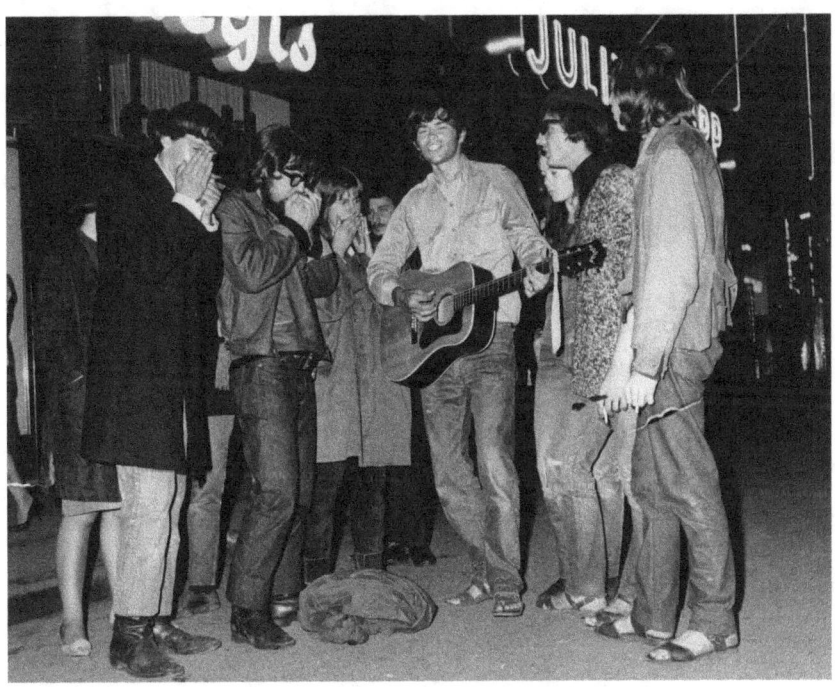

Street singing with friends on Strøget, Copenhagen's famous walking street, 1964.

WILLIAM BURROUGHS & SCIENTOLOGY
A FIRST HAND ACCOUNT

I had almost no idea who William Burroughs was when I met him in London in the fall of 1967. I had just graduated from the Fine Arts program at Cornell University and had spent the preceding four years participating in one of the most exciting social transformations imaginable. This truly seismic shift happened quickly and was fueled by psychedelics, rock and roll, and the ugly prospect of the Vietnam War. Bottom line, it was about unraveling life's spiritual secrets and changing the world.

At about this same time, through a friend in the Cornell architecture department, I encountered something called Scientology. I must say that before the acid trip mentioned above, things spiritual were not really on my radar. I didn't know much about spirituality, and if I had thought about it at the time I'd say that I was fairly antagonistic toward organized religion in general. This was probably due in part to my boarding school experience that was almost identical to the one so well documented by J.D. Salinger in his book *Catcher in the Rye*. And although I had no real knowledge of Eastern religions, because of the Beatles, I knew what a sitar sounded like and psychedelic, quasi-Eastern spiritual themes were beginning to gain a footing among young people. And of course Timothy Leary was out there doing a little preaching.

As an aside, let me say that if you ever want to understand at least one of the underlying mindsets that the '60s grew out of, you need only read *Catcher in the Rye*. It's there, and although this book will seem quaintly tame in this post-Burroughsian world, unbelievably, this was one of the most censored books of the twentieth century — which just goes to show how incredibly uptight things really were in the nineteen fifties… and beyond.

NEW YORK AND ITHACA

To interrupt the narrative here, I need to say something about the Scientology nomenclature that will come up in this story. When I use one of the words invented by Scientology's founder L. Ron Hubbard, I'll underline it. Then soon after I'll come up with the definition written in italics. This convention should become clear as you read on.

The first semester of my senior year in art school took place in New York City and it was there that I read a couple of Scientology books, took an introductory Scientology course at the New York Org (*Organization*), and had some auditing before returning to Ithaca to finish up my undergraduate studies. I'll explain what auditing is all about a little later.

While in the city, through a mutual friend, I met and soon married a beautiful, gentle young woman who had graduated from Cornell the year before and after teaching for a year, had come to New York City to work in the office of the director of the Ford Foundation.

Before heading back upstate we decided to get married. Even though we both felt that labels of any kind would soon be completely irrelevant, we went ahead largely to please her parents. Her family had spent many years in Ithaca and her father, after rising to the position of Cornell University Provost, had recently moved on to become the President of Emory University in Atlanta. We both knew that her parents would not have been too thrilled about their daughter arriving back in their hometown and living with a long-haired artist/musician type without at least the benefit of wedlock.

It is difficult, especially for young people today, to understand how absolutely extraordinary it was for young men in the United States to have long hair in the early and mid 1960s. It was simply unheard of and having long hair was in fact dangerous in many parts of the country, especially so in the South. This new look seemed to challenge some very closely held sense of sexual identity, among other things, and to say that it was not always well received would be an understatement.

My new wife and I made plans to immediately leave for

London after my graduation to investigate Scientology. We chose London and the London Org because the courses there were a little less expensive than they were stateside and we figured that London's summertime weather had to be better than New York's. Also, the advanced course materials in which we were most interested were only offered in England at that time. I mention these details just to give you a quick overview of things on the front end.

One of the reasons I am recording these events has to do with my great affection and admiration for William Burroughs and his writing. Through some totally unforeseeable turn of events, I had the inexplicable good fortune to meet him, share a house with him, and become friends with him while we were both on a mission to further explore this thing called Scientology.

Also, while it is true that Scientology was and continues to be extremely controversial, it is Burroughs' controversial interest in the subject on which I hope to shed some light. Although Burroughs has published many of his thoughts on Scientology in several articles and others have commented on his interest, I was there at the time of his most direct involvement and I actually understand the subject, giving me a somewhat unique opportunity to add what I know to this under-addressed yet important piece of the puzzle that was the life and times of this enigmatic genius.

More often than not, Burroughs was publicly criticized for his interest in Scientology. I always found this criticism a little annoying and absurd because none of these critics and biographers had any real knowledge of the subject and I guess were too busy to do much in the way of first-hand investigation.

Now let me be clear, this essay is in no way going to be a decided defense of Scientology because believe me, there is plenty to be concerned about and that's putting it mildly. However, even though I have not been directly involved in Scientology for almost fifty years, it is one of the few subjects about which I happen to be very well informed.

Burroughs was and continues to be the quintessential cult figure. Here I will not try to address the power and brilliance and influence of his writing. This has already been done and will continue to be done by others. Nor will I say much about my own love affair with his work. If you are not familiar with his writing, anything I might say would be meaningless and if you are, you don't need my two cents worth.

First published in Paris in 1959 and then in the United States in 1962, *Naked Lunch* burst onto the scene amid the uproar surrounding the book's banning and subsequent obscenity trials. Interestingly, it was the final 1965 First Amendment court decision concerning *Naked Lunch* that was meant to end literary censorship in the United States once and for all.

Upon publication, *Naked Lunch* assured Burroughs' cult status almost immediately and this status only continued to intensify, due at least in part to the fact of his sheer invisibility as a public person. Burroughs felt that he had important work to do and was more interested in doing it than he was in seeking publicity. He was not an outgoing or gregarious person or a self-promoter and, up until around the time I met him, he had for many of those years been a junky, which I gather is a pretty solitary business.

After growing up in St. Louis and graduating from Harvard he moved around a lot - Austria, Chicago, New York, New Orleans, the Rio Grande River Valley of south Texas, Mexico City, Bogotá vía Panama, Columbia's Putumayo River Jungle, Lima, Tangier, Paris, and London. What I'm getting at is that while his work was widely known in literary circles, William Burroughs was, as a man, virtually unknown and it was becuase of this vacuum that the legend would grow and take on a life of its own. He really was, as one of his monikers suggests— el hombre invisible.

He did have some long time friends of course — Allen Ginsberg and Jack Kerouac from the 1940s in New York City, Kells Elvins from his St. Louis childhood, and perhaps his closest, Brion Gysin, a Canadian expat he'd met in Tangier in the mid 1950s. And there were others I'm sure, but at least at the time I met him in London in 1967, in spite of his growing notoriety, he seemed to be leading a quiet life working in relative seclusion.

MEETING WILLIAM BURROUGHS

I clearly remember the first time I saw William Burroughs. I was twenty-three years old and sitting at a table across from my young wife in the second floor course room of the London Org which was located at 37 Fitzroy Street on the southeast corner of Fitzroy Square. This large square was lined with important looking, four-story, stone-faced buildings in the Georgian style, and although our room was not particularly large, it was pleasant enough with tall, east-facing windows along one wall. There were about ten or twelve students present when late one sunny fall morning Burroughs was ushered in by our no-nonsense course supervisor and introduced simply as "William." I didn't pay much attention to this William at the time. He was older than most of the other students and was dressed in a three piece suit. He seemed a bit uncomfortable but sat down and got right to it.

"It" was the study of the human mind and spirit as postulated by the creator of Dianetics and Scientology, L. Ron Hubbard. It was the study of the human condition and how to change that condition through <u>auditing</u> — to be described thoroughly in the next section.

In spite of her Germanic accent and uncompromising manner, our course supervisor seemed quite grandmotherly to me, strict but fair. She did not teach. She supervised the study of the course material which appeared in the form of typed, one, two, or three-page legal size and double-spaced mimeographed documents called <u>Bulletins</u> or <u>HCOBs</u> (*Hubbard Communication Office Bulletins*). You read and studied each bulletin with your <u>twin</u> (*study partner*) and when you were satisfied that you understood it, you raised your hand and the course <u>sup</u> (*supervisor*) would call you up to her desk for a <u>checkout</u> (*verbal test of your understanding of the material*). These checkouts were extraordinarily simple affairs. She would look over the bulletin in question and one at a time, would select various words and ask you for their definitions. She sometimes chose very small and seemingly insignificant words such as conjunctions and prepositions. If you appeared to be uncertain about the meaning of any of these words and <u>comm-lagged</u> (comm is short for *communication* and thus defined in layman's terms — *did not respond quickly and with certainty*), she would say "flunk" and send you back to your desk for further study. Each particular bulletin dealt with some aspect of the auditing level you were training on — level 0. Communication, level 1. Problems, etc.

My wife and I had enrolled in a series of courses where one learned how to audit. Although I do not recall having had the goal to be an auditor, I definitely wanted to gain as much knowledge as I could and thought that it would be a good idea to immerse myself in the subject as deeply as possible.

WHAT IS AUDITING?

All tech or technical courses in Scientology are ultimately focused on one thing: learning how to audit as an auditor, or how to expand conscious awareness by applying the concepts and techniques developed by L. Ron Hubbard. One becomes familiar with the specifics of his ideas and learns how to apply them through auditing.

What I am about to describe are some of the underlying principles and methodology of Scientology. I am going to tell you how and why much of it, under ideal conditions, can produce astonishing results. Is it applied successfully one hundred percent of the time? I would have to say that it is not. Are interesting and life changing outcomes possible?

Absolutely. Can it accomplish all that Mr. Hubbard claimed that it could? No it can not, and although this last fact can be a bitter pill, I do not believe it should necessarily invalidate all of his work.

Are there deep, systemic problems and misapprehensions within Scientology's administrative hierarchy that makes long term participation extraordinarily difficult? Sadly there is no question about that. It is a fact of life that degrades Scientology to the status of a cult with the unsavory overtones of fanaticism.

Should this technology/body of knowledge be broadly understood and disseminated or should it be disregarded and forgotten? Well, as the saying goes, "don't throw the baby out with the bath water." My goal here is to make Scientology -- the good, the bad, and the ugly -- much more understandable and in so doing bring Burroughs' relationship to it into clearer focus.

So what is this auditing all about and why would someone be interested in it? Auditing is simply the following:

1. The action of asking the person being audited (or oneself when solo auditing) a question that can be understood and answered.

2. Getting an answer to that question

3. Acknowledging the person for having answered it— usually by saying "thank you."

Much of auditing is about enabling one to remember that which has been forgotten. The idea is that below the level of conscious awareness one retains memories of forgotten and suppressed incidents of trauma and loss. Also retained are poorly thought out and often counter-survival decisions that one may have made as a result of such incidents, and upon which one may still be operating. By bringing these experiences, incidents, and decisions to the conscious level, one is freed of their effects.

Sounds pretty straightforward but how is it done? It is done by repeating the question over and over and getting answers, thereby gradually discharging the negative energy or charge (a concept taken up in more detail later) contained in such incidents until one actually remembers, gaining new insight. Now you may have glossed over two very important words in that last sentence and those two words were "the question." Through a combination of personal research, experimentation, appropriation, and sheer willpower, the extraordinary thing that Hubbard was able to do was to determine what questions needed to be asked to accomplish these ends and of equal importance, how to deliver them in a way that would predictably produce significant answers.

For me to simply tell the reader what these deceptively simple questions are would be utterly meaningless. They are only relevant and productive within the context of auditing. It is the action of the auditor repeatedly directing the attention of the person being audited that allows cognition to occur. Any guru or shaman worth his or her salt can cast a few pearls, but in the vast majority of cases these insightful bits of wisdom will have very little effect on the life of the listener. It is essential that each person has his own realizations and this usually requires digging deeply — as they say "talk is cheap."

In the mind of the public, Scientology must be one of the least understood subjects around and there are a couple of reasons for this. One is that after the success of his best-selling early book, *Dianetics the Modern Science of Mental Health* (1950), L. Ron Hubbard began to develop a penchant for secrecy. I imagine that this was motivated by a combination of economics and paranoia. The economic upside of secrecy is pretty obvious and his paranoia may have actually had at least some foundation in reality. Hubbard fervently believed that he needed to maintain very close control over the application of his ideas and methodology to ensure their effectiveness.

Another important reason for Scientology's lack of ready accessibility is that it quite necessarily has a language all its own — a heady nomenclature of newly-coined words and abbreviations. This situation exists in almost all specialized fields, with police work being one of the leaders in the abbreviations department. In most cases this difficulty can be easily overcome with little more than exposure and study, but both are required. In the case of Scientology, it is not possible to get a real understanding of the subject by reading Hubbard's readily available books. The nitty gritty can not be fully appreciated unless one has done the training courses and, as things continue to stand today, doing these courses requires a commitment of time, a considerable amount of money, and in some cases at least, the suspension of more than a few preconceived notions.

One of the first and most valuable tenets of Scientology, when it comes to studying anything is this: never go past a word you do not understand. If you do, you do so at your own peril, for in very short order you will find yourself feeling disinterest in and ultimately antagonism toward the subject in question.

For example, once this concept is fully understood, if you were to encounter a student who is struggling and losing interest in a subject, it is not terribly difficult to have him or her locate a point at which they felt good about the subject and, moving forward, find the word or words that they have passed over without truly understanding their meaning. After these words are defined and understood, interest is restored. Now my inclination when I first encountered this idea was along the lines of - "Oh yeah, bla, bla, bla, that makes a lot of sense. I'll try not to do that." Burroughs on the other hand immediately understood another implication of this deceptively simple dictate.

Months later after I had read *The Autobiography of Malcolm X* on his recommendation, Burroughs told me that he was interested in the fact that in almost every Establishment article he had read concerning Malcolm X, the vocabulary used was such that each third sentence sent him back to the dictionary. He was quite certain that the average reader did not bother making this effort, and he went on to wonder if this kind of writing was not intentionally used to cause disinterest and antagonism in the mind of the public toward Malcolm X and his very controversial and in many circles, very unwelcome ideas.

Scientology courses are divided into three areas—studying the HCOBs, listening to taped lectures by Hubbard, and the training drills or TRs as they are called. <u>TR</u> is short for the *Training Routine.* In those days the taped lectures were listened to on reel-to-reel tape recorders and headphones set up in a row. The tape you happened to be listening to depended on the specific course you were taking and how far along in that course you were. Burroughs told me that he didn't think much of Hubbard's writing abilities but was impressed by his skills as a lecturer. Studying the HCOBs and listening to the tapes were straightforward. You were learning about the subject the way you would learn about any subject, by assimilating information. The TRs however were not something that I — or possibly anyone else, for that matter — had encountered before Scientology. Without getting too technical, the TRs are about actually learning how to audit. They are the delivery system. These drills are done in pairs, the two students seated across from each other and taking turns acting as coach. The drills are about learning how to ask a question, get an answer to that question, and how to acknowledge the person for having come up with an answer. It is that straightforward.

One has to learn how to ask a question over and over, in a new unit of time, each time, as though it had never been asked before and to acknowledge the person each time for his answer. This acknowledgment simply lets the person offering the answer know that he has been heard and understood and ends that question/answer cycle. The <u>auditor</u> (*the person asking the questions*) does not care what the person's answer is. He has no idea what the answer is. When the person being audited finds his relevant answer, he or she will know that they have found it and that's what's important. Now an experienced auditor will also know when that answer is found simply by observing the person in front of him. When a person has his realization and finds his answer to whatever particular question is being asked, his countenance and demeanor will change. It might be subtle or it might be obvious, but it is observable.

The E-Meter is a device used by the auditor to follow charge. Charge is negative or harmful mental / psychic energy. I'll discuss the use of the E-meter at some length later. It can be very helpful in the auditing session, but it is not necessary.

The TRs are numbered and are referred to by numbers. TRs 0 through 4 are germane to this writing.

TR 0— is designed to teach the student to be attentive and comfortable just being there in the presence of another person. To this end two students sit facing and looking at each other, doing nothing. Not as easy as it may sound. After the students have become comfortable, the student acting as the coach begins bull baiting, i.e. the coach tries to break the student's composure by using words, mannerisms, or actions he feels might get a reaction. The two students take turns doing this until they are comfortable just being there, doing nothing. The coach may not physically touch the student.

TR 1— is about training the student to deliver a communication to another person in a direct but relaxed and natural manner. To this end a random phrase is picked out of the book *Alice's Adventures in Wonderland* and delivered to the student acting as coach until the coach feels the communication has arrived successfully. Almost any book would do but *Alice In Wonderland* works well.

TR 2— teaches the student how to deliver an acknowledgment that it is a full stop — "Thank you." This acknowledgment lets the person know that his communication has been received. In this case the coach reads a line from *Alice in Wonderland* and the student practices his acknowledgments. Thank you is of course not the only possible acknowledgment. Good, fine, OK, among others also work as acknowledgments. But in my opinion thank you really gets the job done.

TR 3— is about delivering a question repeatedly and clearly in a new unit of time. The student being coached repeats the question "Do birds fly?"or "Do fish swim?"until he can do it effortlessly as if for the first time, each time. Obviously these questions have no particular significance. As with all the TR drills, the skills learned in earlier drills have to be expertly demonstrated.

TR 4— this drill teaches the student the ability to remain focused and composed and to get his question answered in spite of anything the coach throws at him that is not an answer to his question - i.e. random comments and other non-answers. This is primarily accomplished by bull-baiting the student as he asks the question "Do birds fly?" During bull-baiting, the student learns to differentiate between non-answers and actual originations— to ignore the former and to acknowledge the latter.

The abilities gained by doing these drills are for the most part simply the skills that are commonly necessary to communicate effectively with another human being. They are also the necessary skills needed to audit, but they really have little to do with auditing per se other than the fact that they are the absolutely indispensable vehicle on which the success of the entire endeavor rides. They make it possible for the person being audited to discover significant answers.

If you were to observe a room full of students doing these drills, this activity would undoubtedly appear quite incomprehensible, certainly odd and a bit nutty. However if you were to encounter someone in life who <u>has his TRs in</u> (*correctly applying the skills taught in the Training Routines*) you would probably think, hey, that person was fun and easy to talk to. In life these abilities come more naturally to some people than they do to others. Perhaps surprisingly, learning these abilities is like learning any new skill — awkward at first, but once one becomes accomplished, the activity is effortless. Also, although it may seem difficult to believe, when observing someone correctly applying them in an auditing session, the question being repeatedly asked does not seem repetitive or rote.

FINDING OUT WHO THIS WILLIAM WAS

The other students in our course room were a pleasant enough group, most of whom I have forgotten. I do recall one young man from New Zealand who emphatically assured me that his sheep-filled island nation was the most boring place on the planet. Burroughs did not stand out except for his conservative dress.

The year was 1967 and London was a happening place. I recall seeing Jimi Hendrix in a small club that I doubt held more than fifty people. My wife and I sat maybe eight feet away from him, The Experience stage left, and even for a musician-type like myself, I can assure you that he was a lot to take in. When you walked around London you would hear "Penny Lane" wafting out of apartment windows, and

Carnaby Street was for that moment the fashion capital of the world.

Some weeks after William's arrival in our course room, one of my acquaintances around the Org took me aside after the day's classes and in a hushed voice told me that this William was in fact William S. Burroughs, the legendary author of *Naked Lunch* and the father of the Beat Generation. Even though I really knew almost nothing about the Beat Generation and essentially had no idea who William Burroughs was, and was only slightly aware of the outrage and controversy surrounding *Naked Lunch*, I could almost feel the hair stand up on the back of my neck. Somehow I knew that his presence there was going to be very important for me personally and I immediately went out to buy some of his books. I knew I needed to do some homework.

As it turned out his books were not that easy to come by in London at that time, but I was able to find a copy of *Junkie*, a paperback whose cover featured a lurid illustration of a hypodermic needle sticking out of a bloody arm, and a copy of what has become a fairly rare first edition of *Dead Fingers Talk*. Since *Naked Lunch* had also been banned in Britain, publisher John Calder asked Burroughs to create a new book that they could get by the censors. Burroughs accomplished this by adding new material he had been experimenting with and removing the more "offensive" sexual fantasies that had appeared in *Naked Lunch*. *Dead Fingers Talk* was published in 1963 and it remains one of my favorites.

I'd never been much of a reader even during my college years when I had been thoroughly preoccupied with, in a phrase "sex, drugs, and rock and roll." Burroughs' writing changed all that. I was riveted.

I wrote to my mother who was still living part of the year in South Florida and asked her to buy and send me any Burroughs books she could get her hands on. Through the book department of Fort Lauderdale's locally venerated Burdines Department Store, she was able to order *Naked Lunch, The Soft Machine, The Ticket That Exploded, and Nova Express* which she forwarded to me in London post haste. She later told me that when she returned to pick up the books, she was warned by the sales lady who had said in a slow southern accent, and I quote, "Why Ma'am, you know those are sex books!?!" My mother said that she had been quite amused by this, and had replied that she appreciated the warning.

I slowly began reading Burroughs' work and although I found some of the passages to be shocking, I knew that I was in the presence of genius. His intellect was razor sharp, and in his own way he was focusing it on the only subject of any real significance — freedom of the spirit, freedom from "earthbound flesh" and the forces that conspire against this freedom. I had also been surprised to realize that before reading his work, I had never genuinely laughed all that much. Burroughs could be unmercifully funny and I often found myself laughing aloud as I read.

Over the next three months, as I was reading his work

and going to Scientology classes, I got to know William just a bit. Again, he was not outgoing and I was very shy around him. I did not want to intrude and I was definitely in awe of him. On top of that we were all busy studying and learning how to audit. William had opted to take the The Solo Auditor's Course in which one learns to audit oneself on the final levels, including the Clearing Course, (described in more detail in a later passage) after having been audited by a trained auditor on the lower levels. This course path did not take as long to complete in that it did not require the more in depth training that my wife and I had undertaken. I decided early on after that LSD trip that I mentioned, that if there was any hope at all, owing to the sheer distance that needed to be traveled, the road ahead was going to be long and difficult. And regardless of whether or not Scientology turned out to be a viable path, I wanted as much knowledge as I could possibly get, any way I could get it. By 'distance' of course I mean the difference between the intensity and depth of ordinary perception and what we as human beings are capable of perceiving in a state of heightened awareness — the difference between the ordinary and the sublime.

Not too long after we found out who this William was, my wife noticed an advertisement in a London newspaper for a short film by William Burroughs to be shown before the screening of a full-length feature. It was expressly stated in this ad that there would be no refunds under any circumstances, the ticket buyer having been warned that this would be no ordinary short subject.

We went to this screening and loved Burroughs' short

black and white film, *The Cut-ups*. We had never seen anything quite like it before— unique, unexpected, and a bit disturbing. That being said, we were extremely surprised to see the reaction of some of the other theatergoers — booing as they stood up from their seats, gesticulating and in a few cases, actually throwing things at the screen.

We did not stay for the feature and as we were leaving the theater, we noticed a man in a tuxedo in the lobby. He approached us and we told him how much we had enjoyed the film. He seemed genuinely shocked and looked at us as if we might not possibly be from outer space. After a brief conversation, he asked us if we would like to meet Mr. Burroughs. We thanked him but said we had already had the pleasure. This man turned out to be Antony Balch, Burroughs' friend and collaborator who had played a major role in the film's production and distribution. In retrospect, it seems clear that one aspect of this endeavor was an attempt to translate the feel of Burroughs' writing into the film medium. The film is visually nonlinear and the soundtrack is verbally repetitive in the extreme, drawing heavily on some of the techniques practiced during the TR drills, although Burroughs subverts them to his own ends. In my opinion this approach was much more successful in accomplishing the almost impossible task of effectively adapting Burroughs' writing to the screen than was that used in the much later adaptation of *Naked Lunch*.

It was obvious that Burroughs had gained an interest in and knowledge of Scientology long before he entered our course room. Although we never discussed the specifics, I believe he had been introduced to Hubbard's work through an acquaintance of his friend Brion Gysin, the painter and restaurateur he'd met while living in Tangier in the mid nineteen fifties and with whom he had become very close friends while they were both later living in Paris at the Beat Hotel.

SAINT HILL AND CHILLINGSTREET COTTAGE

By the late fall of 1967 my wife and I were finishing up our training at 37 Fitzroy Street and were about to relocate south into the Sussex countryside to pursue further courses at Saint Hill. Saint Hill is an English manor which Hubbard had acquired in 1959 and on whose grounds had been built a series of classrooms which, due to British zoning codes, sported faux, castle-like battlements. This estate was at that time the world wide headquarters of Scientology — aka <u>World Wide</u>. Shortly before our arrival there, Mr. Hubbard had left this headquarters to form the now somewhat infamous and, to my mind, curiously ridiculous <u>Sea Org</u>, housing top executives and devoted followers on a converted commercial ship somewhere in the Mediterranean.

This estate was a couple of miles south of East Grinstead, which at the time struck me as a fairly grim little English town featuring a lot of old brick buildings. It was about 30 miles south of central London. Every business there closed and locked their doors on Friday afternoons and did not reopen them until Monday morning. This seemed quaint until you needed something over the weekend.

We did not live in East Grinstead but ended up sharing an extremely old and charming country house with two other young American couples. It was located in the bucolic, hedge-row Sussex countryside, about four miles south of Saint Hill. This house was known as Chillingstreet Cottage, Sharpthorne.

By the early winter of 1968, Burroughs had shown up and had rented some very unsatisfactory accommodations in East Grinstead which he said he thought were actually haunted. I asked him if he would like to take a room at the cottage and he said that he would.

It was over the next few months that I began to get to know and love William. He struck me as being a rather reserved and shy man, certainly not outgoing, repressed in a way, and always neatly dressed in a suit and tie. He seemed much older than I was, but in some baffling and mysterious way — younger, and, as I had learned from reading his books, certainly hipper than anyone I had ever encountered. At the time he was 53 and I was 23.

I had been studying up a little and would occasionally ask him questions that I felt weren't too stupid. For example: "What ever happened to Kerouac anyway? Answer: "He's drinking himself to death watching over his aging mother in Saratoga."

One afternoon I asked him what he thought about one of my heroes, Bob Dylan. He said "Well I don't think he's saying anything new." I was surprised, but I thought that it was quite likely that he had not listened to this music in the same way my peers and I had. The new music of the '60s was important to young people and we took it very seriously and had the time to really listen to it. In any case, at the time I was too shy and inarticulate to discuss the subject in any meaningful way.

If I'd had the presence of mind then that I have today, I might have enjoyed engaging him in a conversation about how, with material like "Subterranean Homesick Blues," "Mr. Tambourine Man," "Hard Rain's Gonna Fall," "My Back Pages," "Ballad of a Thin Man," "Memphis Blues Again," and "Like A Rolling Stone" to name but a few, Dylan had been able to intuit and give voice to the emerging consciousness of a generation and, by combining this insight with the power of poetry and music, had pretty much single-handedly transformed popular music into a completely new and powerful form.

That being said, I am quite sure that I would have been

the one who learned something had that conversation taken place. Today I think William might have argued that the specifics of the lyrics and what they did or did not address were not the issue. The real area of interest was in the very nature of language itself and the way in which language and subsequently, reason, allow us to manage the world but at the great cost of separating us from — as Don Juan of Castaneda fame might put it — "that dark sea of awareness" that connects everyone and everything. Incidentally, Burroughs had attended a series of lectures in the late nineteen thirties in Chicago given by Alfred Korzybsky, the father of General Semantics in which at least some aspects of this same issue were touched on.

Burroughs did not make conversation for its own sake. He most often simply cut to the chase. In his wonderful small book, *The Yage Letters* which chronicles his 1953 expedition into the Columbian jungle in search of ayahuasca, he makes a typically succinct and terribly amusing observation as he watches a local medicine man croon over the concoction in question: "You can't hurry a brujo."

The ceilings of Chillingstreet Cottage were low, especially for us twentieth century Americans. The rooms were small and somewhat dark, but the kitchen was pleasant enough and came equipped with a giant cast iron AGA stove. This stove had three large ovens and three hot plates with hinged, insulated covers which were kept closed when food wasn't being cooked. The system was heated by charcoal pellets which I added to the combustion chamber every evening before going to bed. The temperatures of these ovens and hot plates were determined by their proximity to the burning charcoal. This stove must have easily weighed 2000 pounds and it cooked better than any stove I had seen before or have seen since.

Across from this stove was a table and two benches on which a total of four to six people could be seated. My wife cooked for the two of us and soon began making breakfast and dinner for William as well. She was a very good cook for a twenty-something American girl, owing in part to summers spent in France before we'd met. She also spoke fluent French. Burroughs raved about her cooking and loved eating early. He disliked the European custom of dining around ten at night, saying that by that hour one was often too out of it to enjoy one's meal.

It was great to be able to share meals with him, and although I can't recall many of the specifics of our conversations, I do remember one concerning governments: "Their problem-solving strategy is the same as that of the dinosaurs — to get bigger." Implying that in the long run they would find about the same amount of success.

Before heading south to East Grinstead, I'd purchased a right-hand drive, 1955 Ford Popular Deluxe for forty pounds. This was a robin's egg blue coupe that, in spite of being built in 1955, looked like a smaller version of American models from the 1930s.

My wife and I were somewhat exhausted after four plus months of intensive coursework in London and had chosen to take Foundation Classes (night courses) at Saint Hill. We wanted to be able to sleep-in and explore the English woods and countryside during the day. Despite this more relaxed evening schedule, it was not long after his arrival at Chillingstreet that I began driving William into his classes each morning. Before I took over, he'd been catching a ride with a young man driving a Mini Cooper into which five people had to be squeezed. This would have been fine except for the fact that this car had to be driven at truly frightening and dangerously high speeds down blind-cornered country lanes hardly wide enough to allow two small vehicles to pass each other. This speed was necessary because if one were late for class, a chit or demerit was given for tardiness. These chits could add up, and even such minor infractions could result in some rather tiresome ethics consequences— which I will describe later. And Burroughs hated receiving them. The reason for these early morning, death-defying runs was no secret: as William sat by the front door dressed in his suit, his hat in his lap and briefcase at his side, and with others in the group assembled and ready to leave, the driver's girlfriend would as often as not wander into the room half-dressed, clearly running a little late.

William did however manage to extract some small measure of satisfaction from her before it was over. One quiet weekend morning as my wife and Bill and I were having breakfast at the kitchen table, the young lady in question eased into the room dressed in a barely closed négligeé. Her dark hair was long and wavy, almost covering her face. She looked down into the cup she was holding and said that she thought she could survive on a diet consisting exclusively of semen and black coffee.

We pretended not to take much notice, when she then began to tell us that she was planning a wonderful party for her boyfriend's birthday. After going over some of the details, she asked us if we would like to contribute financially to her party plans. I was surprised when William reached into his pants pocket and pulled out two large coins. Then, swiveling around on the bench in her direction and reaching over, to my astonishment, he dropped these coins — with a small splash — into her half full cup of coffee. Then returning to the position he had been in and with his head lowered, his body convulsing rhythmically, and with lips pressed tightly together, he began emitting high pitched chirping sounds. It took me a moment to realize that he had cracked himself up completely and was trying to control his involuntary laughter. In my experience at least, this was a pretty rare occurrence and I marveled at the moment. William was normally so reserved that I could hardly believe what he had just done and it was nice to see him enjoying himself so immensely.

Burroughs put a higher value on physical dexterity than he did on brute strength, but at this point in his life I thought he was just a tiny bit clumsy. I remember wrestling with him on more than one occasion where, with feet spread apart and planted firmly on the ground, right feet touching, right hands clasped, we tried to pull each other off balance. He had various strategies that he swore by, but none of them were particularly effective. One featured a "rubbery arm." I usually let him win. I also remember vying with him in the kitchen for the opportunity to try opening a jar whose lid was struck.

For reasons I do not fully understand, one of the overriding feelings I developed for William was that of wanting to look after and protect him. Once I went into his room at the cottage to see if it needed straightening up or sweeping, but it was immaculate, slippers beside the bed, notepad and pencils on the nightstand, typewriter on a small table by the window. When I asked him about the notepad he explained that he liked to make notes about his dreams while they were still fresh in his mind.

As winter became spring, Burroughs finished his training at Saint Hill and made his way up to the newly opened Advanced Org in Edinburgh, Scotland. On June 15, 1968 he officially became Clear 1163. *The Advanced Org* or <u>AO</u> as it is called, was the only place that upper level material was being offered at that time and he was the 1163rd person to successfully complete the Clearing Course. Clear is defined later in this essay when I take up auditing in more detail. His photo and accompanying story were featured in *Scientology's Advance Magazine, Issue 2, Volume 1.*

THE SUMMER OF 1968

From time to time during the summer of 1968, my wife and I would take the train up to London to visit William in his apartment at number 8 Duke Street, St. James. On our arrival it was always the same. Ring the intercom... "Come on up." He would invariably be by himself dressed in a suit or sports coat and slacks. It was a modest but modern apartment with a kitchenette opening onto the dining/living room area. This was a decent sized room and well lit by east facing windows. There was an Orgone Accumulator in the entry hallway, a testament to his long-standing interest in Wilhelm Reich.

Once while the three of us were sitting around in the living room, he asked if we thought he had soul. I asked, do you mean like James Brown soul? He said yes, and after a short pause, I told him that I didn't think so. He thought for a moment and said that it really wasn't a quality he admired much. I was somewhat skeptical about this comment at the time and now looking back, I wonder if he wasn't pulling my leg. Although his face had been dead serious, I think that maybe he might have just wanted to have some fun with such an obviously preposterous idea and that I was too dense to pick up on it.

One morning, after spending the night at Duke Street, William decided to make us breakfast and in the process demonstrate a way of poaching eggs. Standing over a saucepan in which he had boiled water, he stirred vigorously creating a whirlpool effect. Into this vortex he broke an egg, the theory being that the egg would be held together by the swirling water long enough to congeal and be lifted out of the pot in one piece. Although this particular demonstration did not prove to be completely successful, he still liked the idea and assured us that it did work.

We would occasionally walk out to dinner at an inexpensive Indian restaurant just off Piccadilly Circus. William didn't have a lot of patience when it came to bad service and would grumble about it. I recall one evening walking down the crowded Piccadilly sidewalk after leaving the restaurant. Although the sun had gone down, it was not dark yet and suddenly William was out in front of us. He was moving quickly, if somewhat awkwardly through the pedestrians, making karate-like chopping movements with his hands. I found this to be somewhat disconcerting in that I felt I'd have to come to his defense if he inadvertently hit someone.

On another occasion when I'd gone up to London to do some auditing, I spent the night at Burroughs' place. His longtime and I think dearest friend, Brion Gysin was also there. They got along famously. Brion was at ease, playfully giving William a hard time about one thing or another.

Ian Sommerville was also there. He was a skinny blond English kid, a few years older than I was and with whom Burroughs had an on-again, off-again, sometimes difficult, romantic relationship. Burroughs was impressed with Ian's mathematical aptitude, organizational skills, and his facility with sound recording equipment —something with which Burroughs was then experimenting. William took it pretty hard when some years later Ian was killed in an automobile accident.

As the evening wound down, Brion and Ian were horsing around in the living room and being pretty loud. The daybed on which I was going to be sleeping was in that room and it was getting late. Burroughs turned in. A few minutes later he appeared at the edge of the room and asked if, considering the racket, I wanted to share the large bed in his room. In spite of my great and true affection for him, I knew that I dared not, but neither did I want to somehow embarrass him in front of his friends. I immediately and as casually as I could said, "Oh no, it's cool. I'm okay here. Thanks." He shrugged a little and turned back down the hall. From here, looking back, I think

I might have made a different decision.

I envied Brion's easy relationship as equals. At the time I felt that being so much younger I could never aspire to that kind of friendship. To me William was the hippest guy going, yet always the consummate gentleman.

BURROUGHS' INTEREST IN SCIENTOLOGY

Most of Burroughs' friends, associates and critics could not understand why he was interested in Scientology and his interest seemed to annoy them to no end. The short answer is that in a field hip-deep in absurd, ineffective crap, Scientology is not all bullshit, far from it, and Burroughs was smart enough and open enough to recognize that. He was interested most fundamentally in freedom— freedom in the affairs of daily life and freedom of the spirit. And he was interested in unmasking whatever it might be that conspired against that freedom. He was interested in the unvarnished truth, which in Scientological parlance is defined as the exact time, place, form, and event.

I think another reason for his interest was the fact that some aspects of his life were a mess and he knew it. He had his own demons that he wanted to understand and be rid of. For Christ's sake, this was a man who, while living in Mexico City in 1952, accidentally put a bullet through his wife's forehead during a drunken, William Tell-inspired party trick. Awful shit happens and he wanted to know exactly why.

Scientology evolved out of Dianetics, and Dianetics is pretty straight forward. Hubbard's underlying premise is that in states of unconsciousness and semi-consciousness people record and retain memories of experiences or incidents containing pain and loss. Hubbard called these incidents <u>engrams</u> and <u>secondaries</u> until they are recalled and brought into conscious awareness, the information they contain can negatively influence one in the present. Put simply, the auditor can locate such an incident by just asking the <u>preclear</u> (*the person being audited*) to recall one.

By having the preclear describe the incident repeatedly, more and more details are recalled and the negative energy contained therein can be gradually dissipated. These incidents usually exist in <u>chains</u> - *a series of somehow related earlier-similar memories*. Following these chains back in time until the <u>basic</u> (*first one on that chain*) is contacted and desensitized is the goal. It is thought that these engram chains even extend into past lives. The trick or genius here is that by simply asking a person to remember such incidents and by having him or her recall each incident in detail again and again, the negative energy and the effect that this energy has on the nervous system can be dissipated, allowing new insights to emerge.

The <u>auditor</u> (*the person asking the question*) does not judge or converse or speculate about responses. It is the auditor's focused presence directing the preclear's attention that allows the process to be successful. As more and more of the negative energy contained in these incidents is discharged (*dissipated*), the easier it is to recall others. An extreme example of these kinds of incidents and their effects on people can be found in the condition now commonly referred to as post-traumatic stress disorder or PTSD.

This activity is not rocket science. When done well it appears to be the simplest, most natural thing you could imagine and yet it can be quite challenging because the energy encountered is real and can be highly charged. These incidents are powerful and often difficult for the preclear to confront, so the auditor must be present, persistent, calm, and singularly focused. In other words it is essential that he expertly uses the skills he has acquired via the TR drills.

During the process of going through these incidents, many thoughts, emotions, and considerations may come to the preclear's mind. One of the biggest mistakes an auditor can make is to take up random thoughts and emotions believing that they are relevant. Addressing extraneous things that come up during an auditing session is counterproductive in the extreme and is one of the reasons that psychoanalysis and other such therapies are extremely time-consuming and generally not very effective. Burroughs understood all this and had been impressed by the results he had personally experienced during auditing. Burroughs was a pragmatist. He was looking for results and could not have cared less what other people thought about where his interests took him or what he was doing.

Although Scientology uses many of the same auditing techniques used in Dianetics for locating and destimulating specific incidents of pain, loss, and unconsciousness, Scientology, which is defined as the study of knowing how to know, is a different kettle of fish altogether. Through his unique understanding of the human mind and the human condition, Hubbard developed a series of questions that direct the preclear's attention, allowing him to discover forgotten and buried considerations and decisions that are inappropriate in the present and usually self-defeating.

A <u>preclear</u> or <u>PC</u> is defined as *anyone being audited who is not a clear,* but really anyone participating in auditing. While there are several somewhat elaborate definitions of <u>clear</u>, one that I like compares the mind to an adding machine— it will continue to add in outdated entries, giving inaccurate results to new calculations until the clear key is pressed, eliminating old and inapplicable data. A <u>clear</u> is *a person who, through Scientology auditing,* theoretically at least, *is no longer operating on old, uninspected data.* I think Burroughs found it somewhat ironic and amusing that his grandfather had famously invented the first reliable adding machine.

The Clearing Course is *the final auditing level before the OT Levels*, which I will touch on in a moment. I have known many people who have completed the Clearing Course and all the prerequisite auditing that leads up to it. By and large these people exhibit a somewhat unique and often very pleasing mindset/persona/sense of humor. However, I must say that if push comes to shove, some Clears seem a little clearer than others. And in a few cases that come to mind, people who were jerks before auditing remained jerks after auditing. Of course that doesn't mean to say that they didn't feel better about it all. In that 1968 edition of *Advance Magazine* of which I am happy to have a copy, Burroughs, after finishing the Clearing Course, is quoted as saying, "Things you've had all your life, things you think nothing can be done about— suddenly they're not there anymore!"

Not long before Burroughs completed the Clearing Course, Hubbard came up with some new solo auditing materials. These he called the OT Levels. OT stands for operating thetan. Thetan is Hubbard's term for *the spirit, the most basic you — the being that is inhabiting the body*. An OT would be a being who can operate: that is, *have cause over matter, energy, space, time and thought, regardless of whether he is inhabiting a body or is exterior to the body*. The goals of these new auditing levels were a pretty tall order, but extremely enticing and motivating to anyone interested in these matters.

Burroughs completed OT 1 before running afoul of <u>The Church</u> (*aka Scientology after being re-branded as a religion*) by experimenting with certain aspects of the auditing processes. For example, after successfully running the Clearing Course materials in English as presented, he noticed that he continued to get reads on the E-Meter when he ran the same material in Spanish. This kind of thing was a no-no for sure and not tolerated. *Anyone deviating from prescribed procedure* is labeled a <u>squirrel</u>. I always found this label mildly endearing and amusing— some of the repercussions of being so labeled however are not.

THE BEGINNING OF THE END

Predictably, within a year or so of William's completion of the Clearing Course, his relationship with The Church had deteriorated. He was assigned the <u>Condition of Treason</u> (more about this further on in the text) shortly after challenging Mr. Hubbard to make his secret materials freely available so that they could be openly evaluated and put to use by anyone who was so inclined. Although this public challenge was never specifically addressed, the reason usually given for the strict secrecy of these materials is that they are too dangerous to be viewed by the unprepared — sickness or even death being possible outcomes. While it is true that even the most profound insights are usually wasted on someone who has little or no understanding of the issues being addressed, I think in this case "sickness and death" always seemed way over the top to me and I've never heard of such a case.

Burroughs was born with a built-in bullshit detector that was at least as sensitive as L. Ron's E-Meter (L. Ron is an *unauthorized nickname for Mr. Hubbard*). He felt strongly that true *scientific* investigation into this most important area of human interest should be open to broad study, testing, and corroboration. Burroughs realized early on that as science, even quasi-science, Dianetics and Scientology had a great deal to offer, but that Hubbard's decision to couch Scientology in religious terms was a recipe for disaster.

Although Scientology deals with all the big issues that are the hallmarks of religion, Burroughs felt that Hubbard had chosen the religion-route not because he was in any way enamored with religion per se but because, on the one hand, he wanted to secure Scientology's tax exempt status and on the other, the constitutional protections religions enjoy. Burroughs' objection to this religion strategy was that he knew it would ultimately lead directly to the exact same fanatical mindset that fueled the Inquisition in Christianity and Jihad among Islamists — when you question "My God's Word," excommunication and much much worse are suddenly on the table.

The inhumanities men have inflicted upon one another in the name of religion should certainly give any sane person serious pause. Furthermore and more importantly, religions have just not produced much in the way of results. They have inspired some nice art and architecture, and they have discouraged cannibalism. But really, considering the amount of energy and treasure invested, people should expect and indeed demand a great deal more. Burroughs was interested in Dianetics and Scientology because they were results oriented, and in their own unique way, they were more or less scientific. When Hubbard decided to clothe his ideas in the trappings of religion, Burroughs smelled trouble and his concerns would turn out to be well founded.

SCIENTOLOGY'S CONCEPT OF ETHICS

At this point I think I need to backtrack for a moment. As I mentioned earlier, Burroughs hated receiving chits for low level infractions like being late for class because they could add up and lead to some rather tiresome <u>ethics</u> consequences, i.e. being assigned to a <u>lower condition</u>. What, you might well ask, am I talking about? I am talking about Scientology's concept of ethics. Ethics is of course a subject that existed long before L. Ron Hubbard got his hands on it. What he did however was break down his perspective on the subject and codify it. His clarification is really quite impressive and unembellished, perhaps a little matter of fact, and purposely weighted toward practical application. In Hubbard's view, <u>ethics</u> had nothing to do with things like morality and virtue. *Ethics is about optimum survival behavior whether it be of an individual, a group, or mankind as a whole.* An individual's life is in a continuous cycle of change in which he is surviving or succumbing, or possibly flourishing. Hubbard applied his concept of ethics by breaking it down into a scale of <u>ethics conditions</u>. Once these conditions are recognized, understood, and acted upon, they presumably allow a person to become more at cause over his existence.

Top to bottom they are named as follows:

POWER
AFFLUENCE
NORMAL
EMERGENCY
DANGER
NON EXISTENCE
LIABILITY
DOUBT
ENEMY
TREASON
CONFUSION

Each of these conditions has a formula that consists of actions which if performed lead one out of an existing condition and into the next higher condition. And most of the formulas really make a lot of sense. People who are successful in life often do these things naturally. I will give you one small example: the Formula for the Condition of Non-Existence is as follows: 1. Find a communication line.

2. Make yourself known. 3. Discover what is needed or wanted. 4. Do, produce, and/or present it.

This one is totally straightforward and applicable as people find themselves constantly in new situations be it a new job, neighborhood, school, the list is endless and little explanation of the formula is required. But you actually have to DO the steps for it to work. They are pretty simple.

1- You don't know anyone and they don't know you, so find someone to communicate with.

2- Then introduce yourself.

3 - Then, by listening and communicating, find out what they think they need or want.

4 - Then make that happen.

I can assure you that once you have followed these steps you will no longer be in the condition of Non-Existence relative to that particular person, group. It has been my experience that although you may ultimately be unsuccessful in fully accomplishing step 4, if you truly work diligently, trying to address these real or imagined needs, the results are virtually the same.

There are a couple of other ethics-related items of interest that I need to touch on, and they are the designations of SP and PTS. SP is short for *Suppressive Person* and PTS stands for *Potential Trouble Source*.

Hubbard originally defined a suppressive person as one of the 2.5% of the world's population who are totally incorrigible bad apples — sociopaths. History seems to feature an inordinate number of these types and maximum security prisons house their share. Society tends to recognize these characters, although some go undetected, and most people naturally try to disengage from them, but not always, and often not permanently, much to their own detriment. Also Hubbard considered anyone working against Scientology or the well-being of its followers to be in this category.

Scientology's ethics approach is very clear: in the face of a Suppressive Person you must <u>disconnect</u> from them — *cut all ties*. If the Suppressive Person is connected to Scientology, he is officially labeled as such so that others will know not to associate with him. A <u>Potential Trouble Source</u> or <u>PTS</u> is *a person who is likely to create problems or trouble because they are connected to an <u>SP</u> or Suppressive Person*. The remedy for this situation is to have the <u>PTS</u> disconnect from or <u>handle</u> the suppressive person to whom they are connected. In the case of Scientology, handle would mean *reverse the <u>SP's</u> antagonism toward Scientology*.

Now none of this is too terribly crazy when used in appropriate situations and can in fact be very workable. Unfortunately this is also where things can go and do go very very wrong and get stupidly ugly. Scientology has become infamous for vengeful harassment that, to my mind, borders on the criminal. Hubbard himself became more and more paranoid over the years, and after his death when the organization was taken over by people who were completely ignorant of real spiritual insight, these SP, PTS designations became even more commonly used as vengeful tools of leverage and punishment. The targets were anyone who disagreed with Scientology or its leadership, or any Scientologist who questioned the gains they thought they should be getting from auditing.

"Oh you say you don't feel like you're getting the gains you expected from <u>Level One auditing</u>... (*auditing that addresses identifying the source of life's problems*). Well, how does your Uncle Walt feel about Scientology? Doesn't like it eh? Well Uncle Walt is obviously an SP. That's the problem and you are either going to have to get him in here for some auditing and handling or you're going to have to disconnect from him, and by the way, since he is connected to your mother and father and brothers and sisters, and their children, they are clearly also PTS so you'd better disconnect from your parents et al while you're at it, unless of course they are also willing to disconnect from Uncle Walt." In spite of scripted denials delivered by Scientology's public relations department, this is how families were and are being torn apart every day. Also Scientologists at every level, with the exception of a select few celebrities, movie stars, wealthy patrons, and those who are able to fly under the radar, were and are made to endure all sorts of ridiculous humiliations and deprivations in the name of *ethics handling*. Stories concerning the involuntary incarceration of Sea Org members in the <u>chain locker,</u>

originally in Commodore Hubbard's *ship's hold*, are legend.

Now you might wonder why people would stand still for this kind of treatment? For the most part there is one simple answer to this question. Most active Scientologists believe, to one degree or another, that, to quote a phrase that is drummed into them almost from the beginning of their introduction to the subject — *Scientology is the only road to total freedom*. That is: the only road to immortality, to stepping off the wheel of death and rebirth, to Nirvana. This basic tenet is reinforced over and over and bolstered by such nonsense as requiring *Sea Org* candidates to sign a *billion* year contract. As previously touched on in this text, in earlier times there was a fascinating period in Scientology history when the Church sheltered its senior management and upper-level auditing on ships-at-sea staffed by <u>Sea Org members</u>— *Scientologists who'd dedicated all of their foreseeable future lifetimes to this service*. Although the Sea Org to my knowledge still exists and continues to operate a small ship, without Commodore Hubbard at the helm— public relations glossies notwithstanding— I am quite sure that it exists in a deeply bemused and ironic state of being.

You might think that this simply does not make a lot of sense, and yet it is a testament to something quite extraordinary: in spite of the apparent craziness that goes on within the Scientology organization, Hubbard did develop a great deal of fascinating and workable material that actually does address some of the more basic, everyday concerns that human beings have. It is tough to let go of dreams of better things to come, especially when the entry level material has undoubtedly produced some very tangible results. Here I am referring to the lower level auditing that incrementally addresses the preclear's ability to communicate, to identify the source of his problems, to come to terms with things that he has done or not done that he may feel guilty about, to resolve his upsets with others, and to discover hidden decisions that he has made that are counter to his survival in the present. It was the training courses for these levels of auditing that my wife and I began in London and Saint Hill and which we completed in Los Angeles two years later.

The OT levels, on which I hesitate to comment in that I had pulled the plug before auditing them, seem abstruse and less effective. I have known a lot of OTs, and I have seen essentially no behavior that leads me to believe they have achieved the advertised results– such as being able to operate with full perceptics – *actual sense perception of sight, sound, etc.* – while being exterior to or out of one's body.

Realizing that there is the distinct possibility that Scientology cannot deliver all that Mr.Hubbard claimed it could, regardless of the good stuff, can be a real disappointment. Nonetheless the bigger questions remain and whether fully understood or not, almost all human beings, by their very nature, long for that sublime connection to the universe that resolves all things. Sensing that maybe this ultimate connection to the infinite is slipping out of reach can be pretty difficult to come to terms with.

In a postcard I received from William in 1989, he asked if I'd seen a recent, unfavorable bio of L. Ron and commented — "The further in the worse it gets. Sci-Fi and very bad Sci-fi." Although he continued to be fascinated by the technical aspects of the subject itself, Burroughs made the decision to move on. His interest in what he called The Job and his efforts to identify a path or paths to true knowledge were ongoing.

FROM ENGLAND TO NEW YORK AND OUT TO LA

Meanwhile, by the fall of 1968, the British Home Office had decided that maybe this Scientology was not such a good thing and began proceedings to deport all foreign Scientology students. As for us, we were ready to go. It was difficult for young Americans to live in East Grinstead— a place that shut down from Friday afternoon until Monday morning and in a countryside that, although extremely beautiful, literally contained not one square inch of real estate untouched by man's hand. In spite of the charm, I found this man-i-cured state of affairs to be surprisingly claustrophobic. We flew back to New York and decided to spend some time visiting parents and a few friends before going out to Los Angeles where The Church had hastily set up classrooms in which to offer the courses recently exclusive to Saint Hill and Edinburgh.

Before heading to LA we met up with William in New York City. He was on his way to Chicago to cover the 1968 Democratic National Convention for *Esquire Magazine*. For those of you too young to remember, the protest that surrounded this Establishment political event and the violent response of the Chicago police department constituted one of the turning points in the Vietnam Antiwar Movement and are well documented.

Burroughs would subsequently write an article for the magazine entitled "The Coming of the Purple Better One." As I recall, it was the story of a purple-assed baboon offered up as a presidential candidate and manipulated by clandestine operatives (recurring Burroughs characters) at the behest of America's "money machine." As with so much of Burroughs' writing, it seems disturbingly prescient a half a century later.

During the time we spent together in the West Village he mentioned an experiment he was doing which involved putting two people on the cans at the same time. Again for the uninitiated, the cans are a reference to *the small V8 Juice sized cans that are attached by alligator clips to the two leads that come from the E-meter*. When being audited, the PC holds one can in each hand and the auditor monitors the meter.

The E-Meter was invented by Volney G. Mathison after

attending a series of lectures by Hubbard in 1950 and is used extensively in auditing. It is essentially a *Wheatstone bridge that passes an extremely small electrical current through the body and it is the variations in resistance encountered by this current that are registered on the meter's dial.* There is also a knob on the face of the meter called the <u>tone arm</u> or <u>TA</u>, which can be moved *to keep the needle on the dial during larger fluctuations of resistance.* The theory is that there is an energetic field surrounding the body which impinges on the body and that variations in this field are detectable by the meter. Some of this field is made up of mental image pictures, forgotten and not forgotten. It is the energy contained in these pictures and in the considerations that one may have about them that causes the variations observed on the meter. As these pictures are <u>restimulated</u> - *brought toward conscious awareness and addressed during the auditing session,* in addition to observing the PC and listening to the responses, the auditor can assess certain aspects of what is going on by monitoring the meter. In life these pictures and considerations are subject to constant and uncontrolled restimulation.

Example of the style of E-Meter being used when Burroughs and I were auditing.

If you have ever been in the presence of someone at the moment of death, you may have noticed that as the sentient being leaves the no longer viable body, their countenance can change radically. Suddenly, for a moment or two, the person's face may appear years younger as they and their <u>mental mass</u> move away. This is the *mental/psychic energy* that the person has been accumulating and carrying around for most of their life and perhaps even lives. As he or she exits the dying body, this mass moves away with them. It is the absence of this mass that causes the momentary change in appearance. Unfortunately this may be a sign that disproves the old adage: "You can't take it with you."

As I've said, the E-meter is not really necessary for auditing but can be helpful. Since the meter can be influenced by thoughts, pictures, and considerations slightly before they come into one's conscious awareness, it gives the auditor a heads up as to the situation at hand. I have had the experience in an auditing session as a PC when, as I was thinking, searching-around, and trying to come up with yet another answer, the auditor said "That." For a moment I was confused and then he said "That" again and slowly, as if appearing through a fog, an answer came to me that was truly life-changing. What a revelation! Obviously he had seen some activity on the meter that led him to believe something of import was at hand.

Even though this is a legitimate procedure in auditing, the auditor has to be extremely competent to get away with even this kind of subtle intrusion into the PC's introspection. In this case I had a great auditor — Mark

Jones, who had served as a Marine pilot flying B-25s over the South Pacific during World War II and fighter jets over Korea. He seemed to have nerves of steel. He was also Burroughs' auditor in London.

It is particularly rewarding for the auditor to observe a <u>floating needle</u> — *the needle, which is about 2 ½ inches long, actually appears to float aimlessly about the dial on the face of the meter.* This occurs when the PC has had a major <u>cog</u> (*cognition*) i.e. realization that <u>blows</u> (*releases*) a significant amount of energy as *the Not Known becomes the Known.* This happens when a previously uninspected, non-survival computation that has been unwittingly held in place comes into conscious awareness. It's a bit like the proverbial light bulb switching on above the head in cartoons. These major realizations are often accompanied by a momentary lightheadedness experienced as a kind of effervescing energy gently boiling off in the area of the aforementioned light bulb.

At this point the auditor says, "That's it," officially ending the session — the end phenomenon of that particular process having been reached. In this situation as a PC, I have had the experience of thinking, "Son of a bitch! That is it!" The auditor ordinarily uses the phrase "That's it" to end any auditing session regardless of whether or not the end phenomenon of a process has been reached during that session. In the case of a floating needle, the auditor says "That's it. Your needle is floating"... ending the session.

If you are any good with the meter, you can impress

your friends and the uninformed fairly easily. An old acquaintance of mine recently reminded me of something that happened almost forty years ago that I'd completely forgotten. At the time I was talking with another friend who knew very little about Scientology. We were both doing some remodeling work at the time and I'd asked him how much he was paying a young worker he'd hired. He told me that he was not going to tell me because he felt that this information was between the two of them and that the young man had the right to negotiate his wages with me independent of their arrangements. Our mutual friend (a Scientologist at the time) said "Hey, why don't you put him on the cans and find out?"

Our somewhat skeptical friend was totally up for the challenge. Why there was an E-Meter around I can not recall, but I opened the meter case, handed him the cans and told him not to answer my questions out loud but to just relax. Within a few minutes, simply by starting with an arbitrary number like six dollars an hour, and asking him "Is it greater than six? Lesser than six?" etc. and by observing which question got the largest <u>read</u> (*a specific kind of needle movement*), I was able to narrow it down and determine exactly, to the penny what he'd been paying this young worker. I think our somewhat dubious friend had been quite impressed on the one hand and a little annoyed on the other.

I never did understand what Burroughs was interested in that led him to have two people on the meter at once. Perhaps he was just curious. I imagine that one person held one can while holding the hand of the other as that second person held the other can. When <u>solo auditing</u> — *auditing one's self on the upper level material* — both cans are held in one hand, end to end, being careful that they do not touch and the meter is operated with the other. All the levels after and including the Clearing Course are solo audited.

During this get together in New York, William told me about a new book that had really impressed him and he took me over to Strand Books to buy a copy. As the young cashier looked up from his register, I saw in his eyes a moment of confusion, surprise, fear, and joy. He had recognized William Burroughs! I think that this was quite unusual because at that time Burroughs was still able to move through the world with almost complete anonymity.

This book turned out to be *The Teaching of Don Juan: A Yaqui Way of Knowledge,* the first in a series of such books written by Carlos Castaneda, a young anthropology graduate student at UCLA. Via Castaneda's ongoing accounts, this was for me the beginning of a lifelong love affair with Don Juan Matus, Carlos's Yaqui Indian mentor. Of course Burroughs and I were not alone in our enduring fascination with this subject, which could and should be covered in much greater depth at another time. Thirty years later in Los Angeles a mutual friend wanted to set up a meeting between Carlos and William, but as it happened, time ran out for both of them before that meeting would come to pass.

Later that evening after our visit to the bookstore, my wife and I went out to dinner with William and a young painter he knew. During the course of the dinner conversation, this young man had raved about the quality of some mescaline he'd acquired. When he got up to use the restroom, I turned to William and said that I wouldn't mind trying some of this mescaline, but did not feel comfortable coming right out and asking for some. William nodded, indicating that he understood the situation and that he would handle it.

When his friend returned to the table and after an awkwardly long silence, Burroughs blurted out that we would all be interested in trying some of his mescaline. His friend seemed pleased and we adjourned to his painting studio/loft somewhere along South Broadway. There were several large paintings hanging on the walls. They were eight feet square or larger and all white — "the white series."

The painter's girlfriend was there and the five of us dropped the white tabs. For the following few hours we were enthralled by Burroughs' recollections of various science fiction books he had read. He told stories in his own special way and the four of us were absolutely spellbound. In one particularly hilarious sequence, he described a much sought after item on some planet or another. It was called the Happy Cloak— you put it on and it ate you alive.

He recounted these stories in that slightly southern, slightly nasal, midwestern, St. Louis accent that seemed so contrary to what one might have expected. At that time the man had lived in Tangier and Europe for at least fifteen years but there was no trace of that in his voice. His slow, raspy, flat tones gave his dry, outrageous sense of humor an unexpected hilarity. One of the wonderful things about having known him is that to this day, if I listen, I can hear that voice when I read his work and that is truly magical! I don't believe it is possible to fully appreciate his writing without knowing that voice. Fortunately today there are many recordings of him reading and lecturing, and although his voice in these later recordings is not quite as strong as it had been when I first met him, if you've never done it, listening to these recordings can be a real eye-opener.

Earlier that spring as Burroughs was leaving Chillingstreet Cottage for the last time, I asked him if I could record him reading something. I knew that I wanted to somehow hold on to that wonderful voice. He picked up a cereal box and read its back and suddenly it was all Burroughs. I still have that tiny reel-to-reel recording around somewhere.

Although Burroughs is generally and correctly thought of as the ultimate social/literary outlaw, that night on South Broadway as the four of us listened, I have the vague recollection of feeling as though we were children sitting at the feet of a warm and kindly wise man, a benevolent but irreverent sage, and we really could not have loved him more.

Some hours after we had taken the mescaline, William stood up, put on his hat and said he'd better be going. I walked him to the door. It was still pitch-black outside and I hoped that he would be all right getting across town to the West Village where he was staying. Although we exchanged letters, I would not see William again for nine years.

THE BUNKER AND BEYOND

That next meeting took place in the summer of 1977, and to quote my generation's immortal bard "a lot of water under the bridge and a lot of other stuff too." I had spent the intervening years in Los Angeles, San Francisco, Mill Valley, and Berkeley and back to LA, where in 1975 I settled into a then defunct downtown manufacturing and warehousing area about six blocks southeast of City Hall and adjacent to Little Tokyo and Skid Row. Thirty years later this area would become known as The Arts District. Note: once such a wonderfully forgotten and anonymous area is "named," start thinking seriously about somehow buying property or packing your bags. The end is near.

At the time of this meeting I was back on the East Coast

with my five-year-old son and my second wife. I wanted to show her New York. We drove into the city from the house where I had grown up and in which my mother still lived. We took in the sights and visited a graphic artist and illustrator I'd met in England in 1968. He was now living on the second floor of a building at 117 Bowery. While we were there I thought about Burroughs, but at that moment I did not know exactly where he was and had no way of getting ahold of him. After he'd left Duke Street in London, I addressed my letters c/o his agent's Canal Street Station PO Box.

When we returned home the following morning and, after pulling the car up our steep driveway and parking, my mom stuck her head out of her second-story bedroom window and called out that William Burroughs had just phoned and left his number. The happiness and incongruity of that moment are still palpable. I had given William our home phone number years earlier as a fallback, stable point of connection when I'd left England in 1968. That he would still have that number and know to call it on that day seemed like a miracle to me. Had he seen me on the street the day before while we were visiting my friend a few blocks to the south? I forgot to ask him when I had the chance.

I returned his call and my wife and I made the hour drive back into the city the next morning. He was then living at 222 Bowery in a concrete basement space that would come to be known as The Bunker. He was just the same, neatly dressed and by himself. It was great to see him and to introduce him to my wife. Although the room was quite dark and bare, there was enough furniture to serve and we sat around talking about Scientology and England and Don Juan of Castaneda fame. When he asked if he could offer us something, opening the refrigerator, which was in the main room where we were sitting, he seemed genuinely surprised to see absolutely nothing but its glaring white light and a bottle of vodka.

He showed us some of his guns and other weapons, which included a kind of telescoping blackjack made out of three heavy, concentrically-sized metal springs with a steel ball at the end which could be extended with the flick of the wrist. I was fascinated by the fact that it was exactly like the one I'd bought in West Berlin while hitchhiking around Europe. Boys will be boys I guess. He also showed us a manuscript he was working on. I'm not sure which one.

I was surprised when a young man came in and William introduced him as his son, Billy. I had not heard mention of Billy since *Junkie*. It was obvious that their relationship was awkward and strained. After the tragic death of his mother, Billy had been raised in Palm Beach by his grandparents on Burroughs' side of the family. He was clearly a damaged soul.

In the early 1960s, I had lived very briefly in a house my father built on the beach only a couple of miles north of where Billy had been brought up by Burroughs' parents. Although our paths did not cross at that time, I knew the exact spot Burroughs mentions in a piece I read years later, where with shoes off, pant legs rolled up and standing at the edge of Lake Worth, he tosses a weighted bag of empty Paregoric bottles which Billy had imprudently left lying around his grandparents' home while awaiting a court appearance for writing prescriptions on a stolen RX pad. Burroughs describes a Palm Beach police cruiser inching slowly by, giving him the once-over. But all they see is an old man in a suit and hat standing at the water's edge and they move on. At the time he had made a rare trip to Florida to try to help his son in the upcoming court case.

Billy didn't stay around long and after hanging out for the rest of the day, my wife and Willian and I walked out for dinner to yet another inexpensive, nearby Indian restaurant. After the meal we said our goodbyes, figuring we would see each other out in Los Angeles.

It was at around this exact moment and unbeknownst to us, that the FBI was raiding the offices of The Church of Scientology in Los Angeles and Washington D.C. This raid was precipitated by their accidental discovery of "Operation Snow White" — the infiltration of and break-in at I.R.S. headquarters in D.C. by Scientologists. The news reports at the time described this Operation as *"a systematic attempt by Scientologists to steal classified files on Scientology from governments all over the world."* I will not go into the details here because they are more or less documented elsewhere, but when I heard about it, I was equally shocked by the audacity and absurdity of this Snow White enterprise.

I knew some of the people directly involved in managing this operation, and although the press and the U.S. Justice Department made a big deal out of these crimes and subsequent arrests, to my mind, this incident amounted to little more than a group of young people who had drunk the Org kool-aid and who were acting out the paranoid fantasies and orders of a once quite extraordinary man gone off the rails. The long and the short of it was that several people, including that once close Cornell art school classmate of mine and L. Ron Hubbard's wife, Mary Sue, were convicted and fined and did some jail time as a result of the prosecutions surrounding this case.

Burroughs believed that *organizations*, whether The Church of Scientology or The Internal Revenue Service, were dangerous by their very nature, being mostly concerned with their own preservation.

Over the ensuing years William and I stayed in touch and I occasionally saw him when he was out on the coast. By that time his devoted, late-life friend and very effective secretary, James Grauerholz was helping him arrange readings. My wife and I saw him give one of them right around the corner from where we lived in downtown LA. It was classic Burroughs, super funny, and very well attended. I also remember a small dinner party at the Beverly Hills home of a well-known patron of the arts who was one of Burroughs' great admirers. It was always a pleasure to spend an evening with William.

Some years later, after Burroughs's death, I recall

speaking to that dinner party host on the phone. I said, "Stanley, I just don't feel as good since Burroughs is gone," and he responded, "Neither do I." I think this feeling was pretty common among people who had been lucky enough to know him and his writing. Once he was gone you felt a bit stranded, knowing that you would simply have to bite the bullet and carry on as best you could without him. Fortunately, in my case at least, this very real sense of loss and psychic abandonment was tempered by my overwhelming sense of gratitude and good fortune in having known him.

The last time I saw William was in 1990 in Los Angeles at the opening of his *Shotgun Art* show at Earl McGrath's gallery out on Robertson. We stood outside talking, that soft, magical, late afternoon, westside, LA sunlight filtering through the trees into the courtyard. Although we had given up our interest in Scientology decades earlier, at least as a means of achieving our ultimate spiritual goals, he still loved talking about it and old times. I remember him saying over and over again in that voice, "I can't believe he let his old lady take the rap!" He was referring to the fact that although Hubbard had obviously been responsible for "Snow White," he had somehow gone into hiding and avoided prosecution — throwing his wife, Mary Sue, under the bus to do the federal prison time.

Burroughs was old fashioned — he didn't like stool pigeons, cheats, busybodies, bullies, or duplicity of any kind. He was also an ardent believer in minding one's own business and taking responsibility for one's own actions. He has been accused of not liking people, but I think it would be more accurate to say that he simply found an awful lot of people to be boring self important hypocrites, and that was that.

At the gallery opening, I was surprised that William looked frail. Not long after, he underwent triple bypass surgery from which he apparently made a full and robust recovery. There were many times when I thought about taking my young son, William's namesake, to meet him in Lawrence, Kansas, where he was then living, but I never got around to it. Burroughs died in Lawrence on August 2nd, 1997 at the age of eighty-three.

As I recently heard someone say, on one of those British, cold war tv dramas, "I shall miss him all the more because I know that I shall not see another like him." And as my dear departed mother used to say, "Ain't that the bitter truth!"

Although your average citizen does not realize it, no modern writer has influenced popular culture more than William S. Burroughs and his ideas seem more prescient with each passing day. He was brilliant, incisive, terribly terribly funny, and always focused on freedom in all its forms. Burroughs never gave up, never sold out, and never threw in the towel. If I could see a hundred yards, Burroughs could see a thousand and then around a couple of corners. I will always miss, and love, and admire him.

Over the years, I have occasionally encountered William in my dreams. These wonderful experiences often had the feel he created in some of his writing. Although very real, these dreamscapes were places of dichotomy, at once visually random and disassociated but somehow held together by an intense focus. Once I encountered him in a dark and exotic apartment in Paris. Chinese reds and blacks in low light predominated, perhaps a wall missing and perspective altered. In another dream I found him in New York City. It was the quintessential New York he knew and wrote about from the late 1940s and that I had glimpsed as a child while on shopping trips with my father in the 1950s.

Burroughs' presence in these dream-places and in the places he inhabited in the real world gave them an air of transience. He was there, in them, but he was not of them. They were simply places where he happened to be and where he could write. He was always looking ahead, into the unknown, beyond the accepted state of affairs, looking for the isness at the core of reality and it was always such a joy to find myself with him.

In these strange and unexpected encounters we were always about the age we had been when I first met him in London all those years ago. And as he was in life, in these dreams he was always kind and warm but reserved and tentative, and I was so very pleased and surprised to be there in his presence, wanting to contact him on some much deeper level, but as yet unable to do so … and then, just the other night, there we were again, standing face to face. I couldn't believe it. It had been a long time.

For a moment we embraced with a gentle warmth, tears in my eyes… his were calm. We did not speak. Walking together across a deserted city square I am suddenly struck by its silence and say… "Where are all the people? I hope we won't have too much trouble getting over to the other side."

PHOTOGRAPHS
1967-2017

Chillingstreet Cottage, Sharpthorne, Sussex, England

Chillingstreet Cottage was a beautiful, large house in the Sussex countryside located about four miles south of St. Hill, which was itself about a mile south of East Grinstead. The cottage was on a narrow, country road lined with tall, dense hedges. Burroughs' room was in the back of the house on the second floor nearest the viewer. That kitchen I talk about was also in the back of the house on the ground floor and extended into the one story element with the shed roof, far left.

The beautiful young woman in the foreground was my wife, Ann. She prepared the meals William enjoyed so much. She would devote her life to Scientology. I always admired her for her commitment, but her path turned out to be fraught with unforeseen problems. She was a special person, that is for sure.

Burroughs at Chillingstreet. He was a voracious reader and his tastes were broad.

View from the back garden at Chillingstreet Cottage

Our 1955 Ford Popular Deluxe I bought in London before decamping to the Sussex countryside in the fall of 1967.

The carriage house garden in spring.

A view of our bedroom which was in the former carriage house at Chillingstreet Cottage

The positon of the chair in both photos offers an idea of how small the space really was

Yes it's true— elephant cord bell bottoms. This photo was taken in front of the corner of the building where our room was. It's the spring of 1968 in the back garden of Chillingstreet. I noticed on Google Earth that someone has since installed a California style swimming pool and patio right where I am standing in this photo. I'm not sure who was responsible for this bit of poor judgment, but I have my suspicions.

Hubbard College of Scientology

Founder L. Ron Hubbard

Saint Hill Manor
East Grinstead
Sussex, England

Cable: Scientology East Grinstead England
Telex: 95176 H C O Sthil Egstd.
Tel. East Grinstead 24571-2-3

A. Fred Bare
ATTESTATIONS i/c
17/4/68

William Burroughs
cl. Solo Course.

Dear William,

Congratulations on Clearifying on Solo Course.

Nice work, William.

Best,
A. Fred Bare

Church of Scientology of California
(A Non-Profit Corporation in U.S.A. Registered in England)

JULIA LEWIS SALMEN (U.S.A.), PRESIDENT FOR U.S.A.   KENNETH G. URQUHART, PRESIDENT FOR U.K. & COMMONWEALTH
KENNETH M. SALMEN (U.S.A.), VICE PRESIDENT   MARY LONG, VICE PRESIDENT   JOAN DE VEULLE, RESIDENT AGENT (ENGLAND)
DENNY L. FIELDS (U.S.A.) SECRETARY   MONICA QUIRINO, SECRETARY

Burrough's cerificate of completion of his solo auditing course

In this photo taken in the early fall of 1968, I am reading that copy of *The Teachings of Don Juan: A Yaqui Way of Knowledge* that I'd bought with William at the Strand in New York City a few days earlier. My wife and I were visiting my friend Robin Williams from college who had just graduated with a degree in architecture. He and his wife were in Bennington Vermont assisting the artist Kenneth Noland. Noland had a summer place there which included a nice old farm house with a big studio in the barn. He also had a nice collection of paintings hanging in the living room. I specifically recall an early Mondrian, a long, narrow, horizontal Morris Louis, and a super simple Picasso line drawing in pencil that really stood out. Robin told me that he would sometimes get a call from Kenneth down in New York City asking him to drive that Picasso drawing into town. He missed it that much. Really great art is like that and it is a pretty scarce commodity.

We finished our courses in 1969 and moved to the Bay Area. We were broke and staying with friends in Mill Valley. After working in a production cabinet shop for a few months, I built this pretzel cart and began a business selling east coast style soft pretzels on the sidewalk in front of Sproul Plaza at the entrance of UC Berkeley. I named the cart "Bill's Naked Lunch Room"

I've kept my connection to music, playing with friends, or solo, as circumstances have presented themselves. In the 80's I began playing more when my longtime friend, an accomplished musician and bass player, came to live with us. We would play nearly every night before dinner.

Summer 1977

Bunny standing in front of 117 Bowery where we were visiting Sandy Hoffman, the graphic artist I'd met in England in 1968 when he was on his way back from touring Morocco in his Porsche 911 he'd bought in Germany. Later that day Burroughs called my mother and left his number.

Willliam and I standing outside of 222 Bowery in Lower Manhattan aka The Bunker.

I appear to have just wandered off the set of *Saturday Night Fever*. This photo was taken sometime in the summer of 1977 by my wife, Bunny in front of 222 Bowery in Lower Manhattan. This was Burroughs residence after he finally, permanently, gave up his apartment at 8 Duke Street, St. James, London. This was a basement space but may have had a couple of clearstory windows. It was quite dark and would come to be known as The Bunker. He was most definitely famous and recognizable by this point in his life and this new Manhattan location made him much more accessible. From what I understand, it wasn't long before quite a scene swirled around him there until James Grauerholz and a rent increase convinced him to relocate to Lawrence, Kansas.

Our loft at 607 East Third Street, Los Angeles where Bunny, Will and I lived in the mid-Seventies.

Bunny and I scouting the desert Southwest about 2000. I could go on and on, but once again I think our body language says it all.

This is the gallery out on N. Robertson Blvd. where I saw William for the last time in September,1990... where we stood chatting in that tree shaded courtyard behind the white wall.

800 Traction Avenue, Los Angeles, California

I lived at this address on Traction from 1978 until 2017, basically my entire adult life. It was a great run and we helped create a great community, but nothing lasts forever.

CORRESPONDENCE
1969-1989

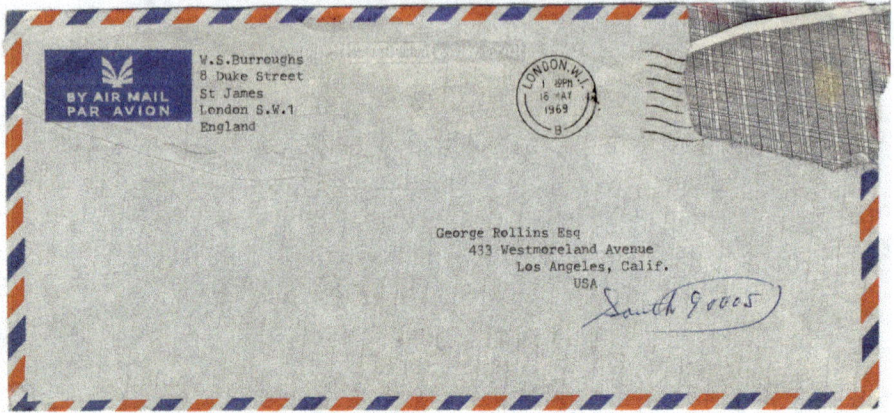

May 15, 1969
8 Duke Street.
St James
London S.W.1

Dear George:

Glad to hear from you. The treason order has been lifted on a written promise to be more careful in the future. On the other hand they have no objection to the expression of opinions. Seems like the organization is getting a more liberal look.
I have been working on a film script of Dutch Schultz's life. My new book called The Job will be out in September. Brion book The Process is already out and a real gas. A lot in it about the early scientologists. There is a book called The Mind Parasites by Colin Wilson that is a real must for all scientologists. Shows what the auditor is really up against.

All the best to you and Anne

Love
Bill
Bill Burroughs

September 1, 1969
8 Duke Street
St James
London S.W.1

Dear George:

Nice to hear from you. It seems that Scientology is getting a new look. They put me in a condition of treason at one point and when I refused to change my position they removed the order.
I hear from Mark Jones from time to time. He has a franchise and is doing well.
Did you ever get Brion's book? It is published by Double Day and I am sure you could order it from any book shop. Some very interesting side lights on the early days of Scientology. I am coming to New York at the end of this week to write a shooting script on my Dutch Schultz film.
Glad to hear you say that most of the people who attest OT are not OT at all. One of the points that got me in a condition was just that. I said that these people who go clear in two hours are not clear and have not run the material. I dont think that everyone can be an OT.
Ever seen a tone arm at flat 0? That's where mine is now most of the time. Dont know what this means. Any case feeling fine and getting a lot of work done.
Have you seen this paper called Freedom Scientology? My God. It certainly isnt doing them any good. This John Birch sound. And the minister of health is suing them for defamation of character. I feel that sitting on the fence and trying to placate the reactionaries is simply not a workable policy. I would like to see them come out for the students who are fighting for freedom if anybody is. In fact I told them as much and they said I had a right to my opinion which as I say is a more liberal attitude than they have shown in the past

All the best to you and Anne
William S. Burroughs
William S. Burroughs

W.S.Burroughs
8 Duke Street
St James
London S.W.1
England

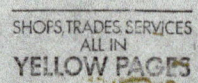

George and Anne Rollins
143 Morningsun Ave
Mill Valley, Calif 94941
USA

May 4, 1970
8 Duke Street
St James
London S.W.1
England

Dear George and Anne:

Sorry to be slow about writing. I have been in Paris and Tangier.

You may have seen my article in the LosAngeles Free Press on

Scientology. Marry Sue and L Ron Hubbard have both written answers

to it which I have in turn answered and also a long letter in the

Free Press by some one named Mustain. All missing the point completely.

My Book THE JOB will be out in the states published by Grove Press

on May 15. ~~Quiet~~ Quite a lot about Scientology.

Please write and let me know what you are doing

All the best to you

William
William S Burroughs

William S. Burroughs
P. O. BOX 842 · CANAL STREET STATION
NEW YORK, N. Y. 10013

George Rollins

607 East 3rd Street

Los Angeles CA 90013

WILLIAM S. BURROUGHS

Jan. 23,1977

Dear George:

It was graet to hear from you and many thanks for the photos. Gather you are doing OK. My secretary James Grauerholz who plays guitar is fascinated by the Energy Bow.

I had'nt heard about Quinten Hubbard and have no clear idea as to which son this is. Was it an OD? I have had no contact with Scientology in a long time years in fact. Did run into an old timer who was taking my course at the Naropa Institue in Boulder Colo. Despite having been purged many times he is in correspondance with El Ron who is living quietly in Florida on his to my mind somehwat dubiously gotten gains.

I travel a lot these days giving lectures and readings. Have been to the coast several times mostly San Francisco and Berkeley. Will certainly look you up if I get to LA and hope you will do the same if you touch down here.

Please let me hear from you again.

All the best for 77

from
William Burroughs

P. O. BOX 842/CANAL STREET STATION /NEW YORK, N. Y. 10013

This from 1986. I was having breakfast with my Mom, watching lift-off the morning of the-ill fated Challenger launch which William refers to in this card. Hubbard could not have been further from my mind. William uses my Traction Avenue address here.

Post card from Burroughs that reads:

Dear George,

Have you seen the two bios of El Ron? one by his son. Both completely unfavorable. The further in the worse it gets. Sci- Fi and very bad Sci-Fi. Do keep in touch. thank for your card

Love,

William S Burroughs

LSD...WAKING UP
1966 - THE TRIP THAT CHANGED EVERYTHING

LSD-25, lysergic acid diethylamide, was discovered in 1938 by the Swiss chemist Albert Hoffman while working in the pharmaceutical-chemical department of Sandoz Laboratories in Basel, Switzerland. Hoffman would later go on to isolate psilocybin, the name he gave to the active compound found in psilocybe mexicana, commonly referred to as magic mushrooms. Hoffman's book *LSD - My Problem Child. Reflections On Sacred Drugs, Mysticism, and Science* is a must-read for anyone interested in the subject. Aldous Huxley's *Doors of Perception* is a related classic.

One year before meeting Burroughs, I experienced the LSD trip that would totally change my life. I had spent most of the summer of 1966 in Lower Manhattan hanging out at a friend's painting studio. It was located on Front Street in a rundown, three story, brick walk up, just behind the Fulton Fish Market at the foot of the Brooklyn Bridge. I was twenty-two years old.

By mid September a classmate and I had rented one of those New York City semi-basement spaces four steps down from the street on the northside of Ninth between First and A, just west of Tompkins Square Park. It had very little natural light but was quite large, and we were planning to use it as a work-studio and living space when classes began later that fall. It was located on the Lower East Side and the rent was seventy five dollars a month. When I arrived in the East Village, as that area is called, it was the summer before the Summer of Love and there were lots of young people on the streets. In spite of the area's reputation for being a little rough, nobody thought a thing about it. What we did sense was the 1950s rapidly disappearing in the rearview mirror.

Pot and psychedelics hit Northeastern university campuses in 1963/64 and I had taken LSD five or six times over the past couple of years. Although these earlier trips had been mind-bending, they were certainly not life-changing, nor were they unfraught with anxiety.

Toward the end of that summer's vacation, my friend and I had scored some acid from a long-haired, curly-headed blond boy from California. He dispensed the liquid acid from a small brown glass bottle onto sugar cubes with an eyedropper, one drop per cube, and after wrapping each cube in tinfoil, advised us to keep them in the fridge.

On the day in question, I had arrived back at our studio in the late afternoon. My roommate was there and for no particular reason we decided to drop acid. It usually takes a good half hour for acid to start coming on and there is no going back, so we settled in and took turns reading aloud from a paperback by Alan Watts. At the time I was not very familiar with what he was talking about, but I think we both found it soothing. Before long, as the type we were reading began, as Burroughs describes, "to dissolve into an indecipherable mosaic," the acid began coming on strong. This was sometimes referred to as 'coming on like a freight train,' but, to again quote Burroughs, I think the phrase — like a powerful, "vibrating, soundless hum" would be much more accurate.

We felt no compulsion to talk and as often happens with acid after it has come on, a physical chill set in. This is often accompanied by varying degrees of anxiety. We both felt the chill but any anxiety was very mild.

Near the middle of this thinly furnished, open space, was a slightly raised, eight foot square wooden platform covered by a few inexpensive Persian rugs. We decided to lie down side by side and to pull one of these carpets over ourselves for warmth. We lay there quietly. After some time had passed, I noticed that it had gotten dark. A handmade paper-mâché light fixture dimly illuminated the room. It was hanging almost directly above us, not too far out of reach. It consisted of a bare bulb surrounded by a multi-colored shade of the kind made by applying overlapping, torn strips of different colored tissue paper and glue onto a blown-up balloon which is popped and removed after the glue has dried. It is completed by cutting a hole in the larger end through which the bulb is inserted and a small hole at the opposite end for the lamp cord.

As I looked at this hanging light I became aware of movement. The colors and shapes in the shade began to slowly undulate in a fascinating, mesmerizing way. It seemed alive. The blues and pinks and orange pulsed with a truly glorious light. I had never seen anything like it. I was so infatuated by what I was seeing that I forgot that my friend was lying there next to me. I am not sure how long I observed this light, transfixed. I then became aware of the fact that, surprisingly, the chill had completely disappeared and had been replaced by a truly wonderful warmth that seemed to emanate from the center of my body. This soothing, softly vibrating, spectacular warmth radiated outward in all directions from some unknown central core of my physical being. Although this sensation alone was absolutely remarkable and inexplicable, what I was about to experience next changed everything.

I began to stir and started moving my right hand up from underneath the carpet that was covering us. As I absentmindedly lifted my hand toward the top edge of the carpet that had been drawn up to my neck, it came to rest on my chest. My hand seemed to somehow dissolve and actually sink in— to merge on an almost molecular level.

This alone would have been astonishing enough but in the next instant this area of contact exploded in soft, exquisite orgasm. I can't really communicate what that moment was like. This experience contradicted everything I thought I knew about the world, and that was just the beginning of what was to come.

In the next moment I became aware of what I believed to be my foot touching the foot of my friend who was lying next to me. My foot was also dissolving in orgasm. I turned toward my companion, and as our eyes met, I asked him if he had his shoes on. He said, "Yes." And I said, "Me too." And it was obvious that we were experiencing the same phenomena.

This wonderful warmth that had begun radiating from the inner core of our bodies— somehow feeling like energy particles— encouraged us to remove the rug. As we sat up, this radiating warmth intensified and our bodies began to visually disintegrate into an effervescence of what appeared to be particles of colored light. We exchanged a look of complete amazement, profound peace and joy— true happiness. We were totally dumbfounded. We both knew that we had entered into a state of grace in which there is no yearning, no wanting, no desire, no fear, no time. There was only peace, plenitude, wonder, and the sheer joy of experiencing the profound love and infinite glory that is everything and everywhere. It was sensual beyond imagining, but without a trace of the sexing that is experienced in the act of sexual intercourse. It was the orgasm of the universe to which we are all directly connected.

As I looked around at what had been our dark, crudely furnished basement studio, I was stunned by what now surrounded me. The world had dissolved into a place made of vibrating particles of colored light that radiated from everything and created everything. The physical universe had become a unified field of silently humming, vibrating light particles. This was no longer a world of solid objects that existed in space. All was one. Literally. There was no difference between the chair in the room, the rug on the floor, or my body sitting on the chair that sat on the rug that was lying on the floor. Everything pulsed and effervesced with no clearly defined beginning or end. Then I, the perceiver of this glorious soup, decided to begin moving around in our basement space, astounded.

I noticed a target painting leaning against a wall. Each of the different colored rings that created the painting extended off the surface of the canvas a different distance. These rings appeared as three dimensional bands of vibrating color… The red ring extended a foot or so out into the "air" and further than any of the other colors. I cupped my "hands," which were also made of these same particles of light, and scooped them through the vibrating rings. The painting's colored particles softly swirled and spilled around and through those that made up my fingers before settling back to where they had been.

We were so happy, bowled over by our arrival in this stunningly glorious, unified world that was obviously the same world that we had always known but had been blind to. The Pointillist painter Georges Seurat's work most closely captures the visually unified field aspect of this world, but is a sadly pale and static, two-dimensional shadow of what we were experiencing.

Eventually we decided that we should leave our studio and venture outside. As we approached our heavy, lock-encrusted Lower East Side street door, we hesitated. Our bodies and the door did not appear to be in any way solid. The universe consisted of vibrating light particles and the same thought crossed our minds in the same instant— was it possible that we could simply pass through this door without opening it? That's how transparent the world appeared to be. However, being unfamiliar with this new territory, we decided to err on the side of caution and open the door in the customary manner. As crazy as it may sound, to this day I am uncertain as to whether or not we could have successfully passed through that door without opening it.

As we stepped out and up onto Ninth Street, we could not believe what we were seeing. It was a place of stunning, breathtaking beauty. The colors and shapes of the parked cars under the streetlights were strangely familiar but gorgeously sumptuous! On the street all was in harmony. The ordinarily grimy facades of the five-story walk-ups that define the Lower East Side took on an ancient tracery of haunting beauty.

Tentatively moving east on Ninth, one half block to the

corner and just across Avenue A from Tompkins Square Park, we saw an astonishing sight approaching us on our right: a fantastic vision of light and motion. It bobbed and burned with light — glorious, bright, swirling all colors. Not until it reached us did we recognize it as an uptown bus. As it passed us in a boiling blaze of light and color, I could imagine a twentieth century burning bush story, only this time the god says "Next stop Fourteenth Street — be prepared to change."

We cautiously crossed Avenue A and entered the park. Although empty of people, I noticed a silently vibrating giant. I walked over to it and reaching out, touched it, my hand gently exploding in orgasm. It was a huge old tree and suddenly, for that instant, we were one.

There was a large swing set in the park and my friend and I began swinging high into the air. I looked to my right and noticed that his body appeared as a blob of colored light particles trailing fifteen foot long streamers when in motion. These light particles would trail behind him and then, as he reached the apex of the swing's arc, would catch up and reassemble for a moment before disintegrating again into streamers as the swing descended.

A little later two young men approached me and one of them extended his hand. As I took his hand, mine dissolved in orgasm. I turned to my friend who was a few yards away and called out, smiling, "Hey, they've got it too!" A moment later a third young man appeared— a friend from our art school. He decided to accompany us and our new acquaintances to their apartment and the five of us walked the two or three blocks further into the Alphabet City neighborhood. Their place looked like a palace— dim lighting, a large, framed mirror, and hanging crystals and rich, soft furniture. We commented on how utterly beautiful it all was, and, surprised but quite pleased, they said that they had dragged just about everything in off the street. We sat down and one of them began reading guys' names out of what appeared to be a small address book, explaining that the particular way in which he spoke each name had significance. I was not paying much attention when I heard the Beatles song "I've Just Seen A Face" from their new album *Rubber Soul* drifting into the room. It suddenly occurred to me that they were not singing about a woman's face but the infinite. After that night I never thought about the Beatles or their music in the same way again.

We soon decided to make our way back to Ninth Street. We were beginning to come down and the sun was coming up. Our friend later told us that he had never seen anyone that high before in his life and had decided to tag along as a sort of unsolicited chaperone. I woke up sometime later that day— changed forever. It took many years to make much sense out of what I had experienced that night.

THE BIRDS and the BEES and the BURNING BUSH

"If the doors of perception were cleansed, everything would appear to man as it is, infinite."

– William Blake, *The Marriage of Heaven and Hell* (1790)

The end of Porn

The end of Substance Abuse

The end of Nationalism

The end of Religion

The end of Self Importance

The end of Significance

Where the action is.

THE REASON FOR BEING

The raison d'être of human existence is the expansion of consciousness. When you ask yourself what's it all about, the answer is the above— plain and simple. We are here to expand our consciousness— to connect with the infinite.

Underlying the apparent, somewhat chaotic complexity of what we normally perceive to be discrete objects existing in three dimensional space, there is a pulsating fusion of form and energy that unifies everything. From ancient times to the present, spiritual seekers and, on one level or another whether we realize it or not, almost all of us have longed to directly experience this underlying order first hand — this oneness that unifies all things —

this fire that burns but which does not consume.

One of the first things to know is that we know almost nothing. It is the assumption that we know about ourselves and the world around us that is one of the greatest barriers to moving forward on the path to a different kind of direct knowing. The agreed upon apparency that we normally consider to be immutable reality is but one tiny aspect of the infinite.

And why wouldn't we assume that we know? Our analytical, rational minds plug along slowly but surely discovering new and fascinating things about our world and the universe in which we live. But in spite of this somewhat comforting and very convincing illusion, there is a powerful longing. It can be desperately urgent or it can be almost imperceptible but it is there and it is the cumulative effort of all of us as human beings to satisfy this longing that creates the world in which each generation finds itself.

I have just recounted my own life-changing LSD experience and perhaps not so surprisingly, what follows concerns two kinds of orgasm — I'll call these "Ordinary Sexual Orgasm" and "Extra-Ordinary Non-Sexual Orgasm."

Although Ordinary Sexual Orgasm seems to be on a similar wavelength as Extra-Ordinary Non-Sexual Orgasm, it only hints at the true nature of ecstasy. This hint however is so powerfully pleasurable that human beings have become totally fixated on sex and its nearly endless permutations and variations, and take it all very seriously. Regrettably, given the current state of means, we are rarely able to make the shift to the level where all things resolve, to a place of plenitude where everything makes sense and there is joyful acceptance and boundless love.

This first and by far more accessible kind of orgasm is defined by Merriam-Webster as follows: "intense or paroxysmal excitement of neuromuscular tensions at the height of sexual arousal that is usually accompanied by the ejaculation of semen in the male and by vaginal contractions in the female."

This seems to me to be an extremely accurate definition and description of this kind of orgasm, although it fails to attempt to describe what this orgasm feels like subjectively. Is it even possible to describe this feeling? Well maybe, but I am not a poet so you will have to look elsewhere for that description if you would like one. I am going to call this kind of orgasm Ordinary Sexual Orgasm. The second and infinitely more profound kind of orgasm I am calling Extra-Ordinary Non-Sexual Orgasm.

These two types of orgasm while very similar are very very different — the first seemingly a lower harmonic of the second. The questions that interest me are: how are they connected, how is this connection possible, and what significance does this connection have for us as human beings.

ORDINARY SEXUAL ORGASM

Aside from survival itself, this first kind of orgasm, the ordinary sexual kind, is the most powerfully motivating force on Earth. It is the experience of orgasm that ensures the survival of the species and creates a relentless biological imperative. This of course works out quite well where procreation is concerned — perhaps a little too well considering the current population statistics.

In different cultures, various systems and practices have taken root that attempt to regulate sexual activity. Within some more insular and conservative cultures, these practices can be quite brutal where females in the population bear the brunt of the savagery. In such societies women are basically considered property and males get away with exercising absolute and unmerciful control over them, polygamy by force being widely accepted and practiced — with a little public stoning thrown in to keep everyone's toes on the line.

In western cultures, monogamy has become socially accepted practice, with arranged marriages and marriages of economic necessity becoming more and more rare. These have been replaced in relatively recent times by romantic love matches. The high divorce rate in these more liberal societies would indicate some fairly serious problems with this system and during the sexual revolution that began in the nineteen sixties, attempts were made to address some of monogamy's underlying dilemmas. Unfortunately, as we were to discover over the ensuing decades, the cost of "free-love" generally proved to be prohibitively high.

In any case this familiar kind of orgasm is there, and you would probably not be surprised by the amount of trouble it can cause. Human beings will endure an awful lot of misery to experience a small amount of pleasure, and sexual pleasure is extremely powerful and consuming.

There is the thinking that abstinence is the way to go in order to avoid this often treacherous area altogether and the best explanation for this approach I've heard has to do with conserving energy. In Carlos Castaneda's books his teacher, the sorcerer Don Juan Matus, makes the case that the amount of available energy that each of us is born with is finite, and that in almost all cases, it is wiser to strategically deploy this energy in areas other than sexual intercourse if one hopes to make any real progress toward a more enlightened state. Although this really does sound like good advice, without a clear way forward, abstinence is not often practiced with much enthusiasm or success.

Almost every aspect of human activity is permeated by the powerful forces of sexuality and its desired outcome, orgasm. Most fundamentally this phenomenon has to do with a very special flow of energy. In ordinary sex, orgasm presents as a physical feeling that is so damned pleasurable it creates an almost irresistible attraction. As they say—love makes the world go 'round.

The subject of sex is vast and is covered elsewhere in excruciating detail so, on the advice of my editor but with some admitted reluctance, I will refrain from making any further additions to this endlessly fascinating body of knowledge and limit my comments to one. Size matters, but only relative size. This fact is extremely important when it comes to simultaneous orgasm.

The reason I bring up Ordinary Sexual Orgasm at all is its unforeseen and largely unexamined relationship to Extra-Ordinary Non-Sexual Orgasm. My comments are intended to focus the reader's attention on what is the most powerful and profound experience that is broadly accessible to us as human beings, but here these comments are intended to be a point of departure.

EXTRA-ORDINARY NON-SEXUAL ORGASM

Although this second kind of orgasm is very similar in terms of sensation, it seems energetically much finer and is infinitely more pleasurable. It appears to be an other-level-harmonic of the kind of orgasm with which we are ordinarily familiar. This second kind of orgasm has nothing to do with ordinary sex or genitalia, but is instead part of a much more profound experience. This is the experience that I have tried to describe earlier in some detail and which can be made accessible through LSD. There are of course other ways to at least move in this direction: meditation, sensory deprivation, fasting, chanting, rhythmic movement, other psychedelics, certain types of yoga, lucid dreaming, near-death experiences, and other extremes, but there is no doubt that LSD can open the door to another level of perception.

Unfortunately, unless you have had the good fortune to experience this flowing, pulsating, orgasmic soup of vibrating light particles and the complete joy and feeling of oneness that this experience engenders, acquiring the motivation to undertake a serious and protracted spiritual journey is hit and miss at best. And even though one senses that there is no guarantee of ultimate success, after such an experience there is the total certainty and the complete understanding that this is in fact where the REAL action is. At the very least this experience brings about the sure beginnings of a kind of inner peace that subtly affects every aspect of one's daily life.

The revelation that was my experience presents a couple of key issues. The fact that this experience had nothing whatsoever to do with ordinary sexual contact was totally flabbergasting and yet there was no mistaking it for something else. The already phenomenally powerful and delightful physical feeling of ordinary orgasm was there, but this experience was indescribably finer, all pervasive, and, although the following may sound positively straight-laced it was not, shall we say, confused by the whole wonderful, glorious, somewhat messy, sweaty business of lovemaking. It was pure and the difference was off the charts completely. And it seemed to occur whenever one came into physical contact with other living things, animal or vegetable. Not so sure about mineral. This experience engendered an immediate sense of oneness that could not have been imagined before.

This dissolving of the physical universe into silently humming particles of colored light was totally astonishing. That night everything in the physical universe dissolved, including our bodies. Normally we have a special relationship to and with our bodies. We tend to identify with them. Some people think that they are their bodies, or some silliness like they are their bodies but have souls. Just in case you haven't gotten the memo yet: You da soul residing in that body! When in a universe where you feel as deeply, directly, physically connected to everything else as you normally do to your own body, especially during and directly after orgasm, something extraordinary happens— your body becomes just another part of everything else, no more and no less, and suddenly what's left is you and it is an experience of pure joy! You have entered into a state of grace. The here/there, me/them duality of our daily, rational world melts away and suddenly you become the perceiver of a universe that is finally whole, teaming with energy and pulsing with something that appears to be a lot like light. Your perception of the world and your relationship to the environment change completely. Your wants and needs become very few indeed.

I am not sure why the particular trip I have described turned out to be so powerfully transformative when earlier trips had not, but one thought that comes to mind is that this was the first trip I had ever taken without a girlfriend present. On these previous occasions there had always been an underlying sexual desire hovering about. The thought was always there— I wonder what it would be like to get laid on acid? Let me stress that in these cases at least, it was my own desire and sexual curiosity and not the presence of a woman that may have made experiencing a truly profound trip more difficult. Those somewhat awkward situations that I had previously experienced were entirely of my own making.

Knowing what I know now and what the stakes are, I don't think it would be too difficult to simply set aside these kinds of thoughts and preoccupations. Interestingly in spite of these thoughts, this counterproductive mindset did tend to fall away as these earlier trips progressed because LSD is most definitely not an aphrodisiac in the normal sense of the word. During the transformative trip I have described, there was absolutely no sexual tension even in a world that began to explode in orgasm.

Here I want to add, in no uncertain terms, that mixing marijuana, which can in fact be a powerful aphrodisiac, and LSD is a very bad idea. The chances of triggering an experience that could be truly terrifying are greatly increased. Marijuana is a sensitizer, period, and many find it annoyingly unpredictable. So I implore you to make a note and to take it seriously.

A second reason for that night's profound outcome may have been that on that occasion my friend and I had no particular agenda of any kind. Reading something kind of Zen probably didn't hurt, but really it was pretty simple: we dropped the acid, got cold and lay down, pulled some covers over ourselves and quietly waited in silence. We did not talk and there was no music playing. I think this relaxed state of calm-waiting was definitely a positive thing.

Lastly, I believe that the other extremely important piece of this puzzle could have had to do with that homemade lampshade. It may have in fact been the key that, slowly turning, began to open the doors of perception for us. The light illuminated the paper maché which was very colorful being made up of overlapping, transparent strips of tissue paper. As overly simplified as it may sound, it was visually a perfect storm. Due to LSD's ability to enrich and enhance visual perception, our attention was focused out into the world, not inward. Sorry all you psychoanalysts, but in the vast majority of cases chewing on what we "think" is way more trouble than it's worth. Generally speaking, it's the same old nonsense everyone else is thinking and not terribly fertile ground when it comes to moving toward higher states of consciousness.

Human beings have an innate sense that there is more to life, that something is missing, and that fulfillment might somehow be possible. All religions, and most retailers, depend on this feeling of incompleteness and longing to sell their various brands of salvation and soap. This is also the reason people take and often abuse drugs and do any number of other crazy things— looking to experience SOMETHING!

It is unfortunate that most governments have banned the use of LSD and yet, for example, do not earnestly discourage the use of alcohol. While there is no evidence that LSD is overly dangerous, the wreckage left in alcohol's wake is well-documented and devastating beyond belief. Perhaps the powers-that-be prefer people just the way they are – confused, fearful, and in the words of Thoreau… living "lives of quiet desperation." And god forbid that someone would want to seek other-level experience! Any truly significant change-of-mind might have a negative effect on corporate and religious business models.

WHERE THE ACTION IS

The most basic, overriding problem facing humankind is the fact that there is no predictable, efficacious way of moving to higher states of consciousness. Religions don't work and by work I mean they do not effectively move people to enlightened states of being. I think this is the primary reason organized religions no longer play a significant role in the lives of most thinking young people who are lucky enough to live in free societies. As Burroughs might put it: "The marks are wising up."

In spite of any righteous insight on the parts of their progenitors, most major religions and their all too often truly loco splinter groups have become stilted, my way or the highway adulterations created over the centuries by power-loving men who have been clueless when it comes to true spiritual insight. The unfortunate but predictable consequence of this being a lot of ego-driven mumbo-jumbo that is the hallmark of most of the ineffective catastrophes we have come to know. Religious fanaticism is the least attractive and most dangerous manifestation of this sad reality. Let's just say that at their best these religions are long on talk, trappings, and ritual, but exceedingly short on results. And sadly, the way things stand —doing good does very little good indeed. Once, many years ago as I was discussing South American religious art with a very wise eighty-five-year-old artist friend who had grown up in Uruguay, he smiled mischievously and with eyes sparkling, chuckled — "Yes, we like our Christ con sangria!"

Even the few Eastern efforts that actually do address enlightenment seem to be brutally tedious and, generally speaking, do not produce predictable, satisfactory results — and certainly not in a timely manner.

On the Indian subcontinent another major religion emerged long before those that evolved out of the Abrahamic musings of the Middle East. And although this belief-system is based on reams of ancient and very cogent insight and could hardly be more different than its Middle Eastern counterparts, it sadly shares their very same underlying problem: the inability to expand consciousness and therefore to fundamentally alter the human condition.

While it is certainly possible for these religions to

superficially affect behavior, do not be taken in by the glitter, the pathos, or the promises... They have virtually nothing to do with expanding consciousness... This is not to say that historically these endeavors have been completely bereft of good intentions, but I think most of us have heard which road these pave. To quote Christopher Hitchens: religion poisons everything.

And of course the freelancers aren't a whole lot better. On the plus side, they have generally done a lot less damage than the majors simply because they have attracted far fewer adherents. There has however been some interesting work done and reported on and it is always exciting to come across these reports and to be able to study and evaluate them, but by and large there has been precious little in the way of truly workable breakthroughs.

And ultimately LSD is not the answer. You will never achieve anything approaching a stable state of enlightenment by taking LSD, and once you have had a truly definitive trip, you will feel very little inclination to try to replicate it by taking more. This experience is a starting point only, but real starting points should not be underestimated. These experiences are extremely powerful and few and far between.

LSD can, however, do at least two important things. First, just one trip like the one I have described can change your life completely and in a very positive way. I know for certain that my life would have been very, very different had it not been for my own LSD experience. Now if you know me or were to see me across the room, I am not going to appear much different than any other relatively sane person. However, one of the things you are not seeing is what I might have become had it not been for that trip half a century ago. I know that I became a kinder and more empathetic person almost overnight. I do not expect too terribly much from my fellow human beings simply because I understand their predicament and when I choose to, I can recognize the infinite in just about everyone. Generally speaking, people don't get under my skin because I know that most basically I have no skin to get under.

Second, you will no longer wonder what life is all about, nor will you have any doubts about what is unquestionably the most important activity in which humankind should be engaged. This does not mean that things like hunger and situations that pose immediate danger should be ignored, or that the wonderful things in life should be avoided, or that you will not have to earn a living. What it does mean is that you will acquire the certain knowledge that there are ultimately no meaningful, long term solutions to humanity's dilemma in the absence of expanded consciousness, and that overcoming the barriers to attaining this higher state of consciousness must take priority if we are going to survive as a species.

In closing, please allow me to reiterate: unless one is starving to death or being shot at, in almost all cases sex is the underlying force that drives human activity. Orgasm is so pleasurable when compared to any other naturally available human experience that its emotional and psychological impact cannot be overstated. Under ideal circumstances and most certainly in the case of mutual, simultaneous orgasm, it can engender a sense of profound love and tenderness between sexual partners ... a feeling of connectedness — of joy — and at least a moment's peace, a moment of transcendence. Unfortunately this level of transcendence lacks true depth, is usually short-lived, and soon overwhelmed by the affairs of daily life.

None of this is news. Almost all of us understand this to one degree or another. The news is that this very same sensory phenomena, unimaginably expanded and without a trace of the sexual, is also something that we as human beings are capable of experiencing. The purest aspects of the physical sensations of Ordinary Sexual Orgasm become more sublime, more profound, more subtle, and all-pervasive. Although this is a totally new and different kind of experience, it is clearly, inextricably connected to something with which most of us are already familiar.

This Extra-Ordinary Non-Sexual Orgasm goes beyond what is normally imaginable— to another level completely. As this phenomenon unfolds, one's body and the world around one begin to dis-integrate. By virtue of a powerful, radiating, softly amplified, effervescing version of the energetic glow that one feels during and immediately after ordinary orgasm, the world of discrete, solid objects located in space ceases to exist. The world becomes one, literally— one dynamic, silently vibrating hum out of which everything flows. By cleansing the doors of perception you will actually see, in real time, a new and very different world and it is a world with which there is utter satisfaction and where you require almost nothing.

I believe that this experience of oneness is the experience of what is often called love in its most sublime form. Ultimately this is the love we are all looking for. This is the love about which the true prophets and enlightened ones have spoken and it is through the lens of this love that they experienced and talked about the world.

For the human race to survive and to achieve its true destiny, we must find an effective way to realize this state of expanded awareness. Exploring the infinite which may appear to be out there will depend on our exploration of inner-space, not outer-space— and that is for sure.

Our personal experience of the love/energy which permeates and unifies everything is limited only by our ability to perceive. Transcendence is real and it is a function of perception. Regardless of your circumstances, enjoy and appreciate each moment, but be aware— Expanding Consciousness Is The Only Game In Town ... and as you may have guessed, everything else is simply the awesome, all-consuming, double-edged reeling of life's dance.

At the conclusion of *Naked Lunch*, Burroughs writes: "the black windsock of death undulates over the land, orgone balked at the post, Christ bled, time ran out." And while this austere assessment may seem even more apropos today than it did when he wrote those words over a half century ago, there is another, very different reality and our priority must be the direct knowledge of this fire which appears to burn but which does not consume. This is where the action is.

It is of little consequence that as yet I have been unable to achieve all that I may have hoped for as a young man. My point here is that with the aid of LSD, I came face to face with a state of being that changed the way I perceived the world and everyone in it. While I do not pretend to have found a viable path forward, I do know with complete certainty that there exists an underlying, all-pervasive, and perceivable light-energy and I want you, the reader, to understand how utterly extraordinary this light is. In *Macbeth*, Shakespeare notes the "sleep that knits up the raveled sleave of care," but as I have tried to make clear in this report, when you are bathed in this sublime light, warmed by this miraculous fire, there is no care— there is only wonder.

Imagine that everything you are concerned about, that everything you think is important, and that all your fears and insecurities are the result of a tragically limited ability to perceive the world around you. While I know that my suggesting such a thing will not make it real for you, I do hope that you might be prepared to entertain such a possibility. The stakes could not be higher.

Special thanks to my wife for her ongoing help and enthusiasm for this project and to my editor for her invaluable work and patience.